MACK'S MOUNTAIN

THOUGHTS

PEACHAM, VERMONT

_____

MEL SOMERS

illustrations

**Sarah E. Graves, Sharon S. Harvie,
Alta R. Sheppard and Ann E. Somers**

First Edition

Library of Congress Catalog Card Number: 2004095730

Mack's Mountain Thoughts / illustrated by Sarah E. Graves, Sharon S. Harvie, Alta R. Sheppard and Ann E. Somers

ISBN 0966519213

file/copypage

CAPITAL CITY PRESS, INC.
MONTPELIER, VERMONT

Dr. Melvin C. Somers

Dr. Somers was born on a dairy farm located in the town of Peacham, Vermont on October 9, 1930. In June of 1939, the family moved to McIndoe Falls, Vermont where they resided on a beautiful dairy farm which was named, "Bonnie View".

He attended St. Johnsbury Academy for three years then transferred to McIndoes Academy where he graduated in 1949. He received his B.S. degree from the University of Vermont, his M.S. degree from the University of Maryland and his Ed.D. degree from Pacific States University. He also attended classes at Brunel University in Uxbridge, England.

Dr. Somers is a veteran of the U.S. Air Force, but spent the majority of his working career in the field of education as a high school teacher, principal, college professor and as a college administrator.

Presently, he and his wife, Ann, are residing at their retirement home located near Mack's Mountain, Peacham, Vermont. They named their retirement home, Bonnie View, in remembrance of Bonnie View in McIndoe Falls, which was destroyed in the construction of Interstate Highway 91. Reference is made to Bonnie View of Peacham in some of the poems.

i

Ann and Mel Somers

I wish to dedicate this book to my wife, Ann. She has spent countless hours of typing, sketching, arranging, encouraging and advising. Without her help there would have been no inspiration thus no creation.

Mel Somers

ORDER OF POEMS

FRIENDS

Life, to me, is like the Mack's Mountain Road,
Where one can walk at a given pace.
There is beauty to be seen around every corner,
A testimonial, to our Maker's loving embrace.

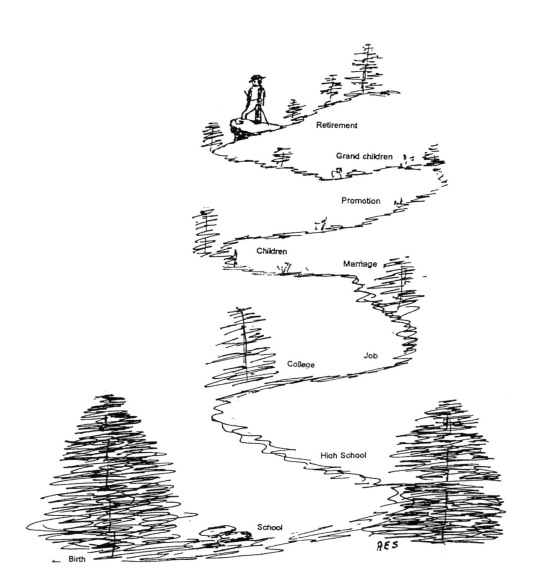

CLIMBING MOUNTAINS

Lord, I pray for a steady hand
And a mind to see the light.
It's guidance I seek to understand -
Your presence is needed, as I sit down to write.

I'm not quite sure where the time has gone
Nor whether I've lived a full life -
But I want you to know I'm more than grateful,
For two daughters, a son, and a loving wife.

There was always room for a touch of envy,
Observing those, "flying higher" than we.
Now that time has provided me a mirror,
I seem to surmise, they were no happier than we.

Watching my children grow and mature
Under their mother's, watchful hand -
Was a touch of grace to be humbly revered,
A lifetime privilege, to a grateful man.

We encountered some turns on the road of life,
Also some hills, scattered with stone.
Guiding young hands to travel this road
Was a two-way contract, before they were grown.

In retrospect, it almost seemed when a problem arose
With a weight too heavy to bear -
A solution came, after due time,
As though in answer, to a heartfelt prayer.

As the grandchildren came one by one,
Each was a grandparent's prize -
But the ingredient that made the picture complete,
Was the love in our children's eyes.

I'm inclined to wonder, as I look around,
If I've really done all that I could.
There has always been another mountain to climb
And perhaps it's time that I should.

MY DAD'S POCKET BEN

I've been to London and seen Big Ben,
Also heard it chime.
It was truly inspiring, listening to its tolling,
As it proclaimed the passage of time.

When I was a boy my Dad wore overalls,
Which were very common back then.
In his vest he carried his timepiece,
A shiny Pocket Ben.

Each night he would sit on the edge of his bed
And wind his alarm clock, also his Pocket Ben.
Us kids knew exactly what it meant,
Where to go, as well as when.

About five A.M. the alarm clock "went off"
Proclaiming the start of another day.
I can almost hear that farm boy's reveille -
"It's time to crawl out," he'd often say.

As we worked in the hayfield, shaking out hay,
Mindful of the sun and its radiant heat -
He'd look at the sun, check his watch and say,
"It's along about noon,
Let's go down to the house and eat."

Later in the day the ritual continued,
Our schedule was governed by his Pocket Ben.
"It's cow time," he'd say, meaning round'em up -
I knew where to go, the watch said when.

It was an exciting day when he got a new watch,
Though I can't remember just when.
It was a brand new Bulova, but best of all,
He gave to me, his Pocket Ben!

AN AUTUMN THOUGHT
AT BONNIE VIEW

I had a notion the other day
When everything was still.
The kind you get when autumn arrives
And your soul has reached its fill.

There's a mystical and susurrant ambience,
That prevails this time of year.
Though you may not see or touch it,
You can always tell when it's near.

Bonnie View has been blessed with flowers
For the past four months or so -
Now the colors of autumn are beginning to appear
As a gentle reminder, it's time for the flowers to go.

As we enjoy a bountiful harvest
From our gardens in the field -
We are thankful for our trip in life -
And for our "Maker" at the wheel.

As the birds leave and the colors fade,
There is nothing, really, to dread.
It's part of a pattern, for us Vermonters-
Rather than flowers,
There will be snow on the ground instead.

My notion was that change is good
No matter what some will say.
We "shift with the seasons," one by one,
And learn to adjust each day."

5

BABE

When my brother, Leon, returned from WW II
He was recuperating from some of its vicious wounds.
For this reason, I believe, he felt freedom and solace,
Working outdoors with nature's beauty and tunes.

He took a job, working in the woods,
To clear his mind from the ravages of war.
It was relaxing for him, being close to nature,
And knowing he would study war no more.

I used to stop by, where he was working,
And he'd show me what he'd done.
He was very meticulous in planning the job -
To where he'd finish, from where he begun.

His pride and joy was his skidhorse -
A beautiful Belgian mare.
He kept her brushed from mane to tail,
I doubt he ever missed a hair.

He affectionately called her, Babe,
And she certainly knew her name.
If awards had been given for workhorse performance,
She would surely have belonged in a "Skidhorse Hall of Fame."

He would hitch her to a log,
Several yards down a winding trail.
Babe would pull it to the skidway, without a driver,
A job she performed and never failed.

If her log caught on a stump or rock,
What Babe did was beautiful to see.
She'd tug to the left then tug to the right
Until her log came free.

Leon Somers
Before shipping out to the
South Pacific
World War II

6

Once she reached the skidway,
She would wait to be set free -
Then return down the skidtrail,
Without a "haw or gee."

He built a snug, little shelter
For Babe's comfort on the job,
Fed and watered her twice a day
As well as grooming, and in winter -
Her tail was tied up in a neat looking bob.

She got to know his voice
As he approached her shelter each day.
He would ask, " are you in there Babe?"
To which she'd whinny,
In a low, gentle and contented way.

Scientists once found the altitude of a star
By using an astrolabe.
My brother's solace touched the highest star,
As he worked with his skidhorse, Babe.

COCOA

Most of the calves, born at Bonnie View,
Made their debut in the Fall.
It was time to "button up" for winter,
We had heard the wild geese call.

Because our cows were Jerseys,
The calves were a light, colored tan.
That is, all of them except for one.
 I'll try to explain it, if I can.

Among all these little, tan critters,
There was one that was reddish brown.
She immediately caught my eye -
As the prettiest I ever found.

I asked my Dad why she was different,
She was obviously one of a kind.
He said "it's the way things sometimes happen,
Although different in color, her lines are well refined."

I was a member of the 4-H at the time
And required to have a project.
Dad gave me this little calf
To which I didn't object.

The local Minister was the 4-H leader,
A just and noble man.
When I told him about my project,
He said I'd have to keep a plan.

The first question was, what's her name?
"Cocoa," was what I replied.
"This was because of her color," I explained,
There was no inference implied.

"What's the Dam's name," he asked,
As he looked straight into my eye.
"I've been taught both at home and school,
That it's wrong for a person to swear,"
I said, which was followed with a sullen sigh.

He quickly informed me of keeping records,
His voice was tender as a lamb.
"There's a certain jargon in keeping records," he said,
"A mother cow is called a Dam."

I remember thinking how he must feel,
After causing my sullen sigh.
He was attempting to make amends,
Or at least he seemed to try.

As you might expect, dear reader,
Cocoa and a 12 year old boy became close.
She learned to lead with a halter,
And learned more quickly than most.

We went to fairs in the summer,
She pulled my sled in the snow.
It was one of the charms of farm life
That so many will never know.

HE WILL GROW INTO IT

My wearing apparel, in my first decade,
Included a few of these and some of those.
Thanks to my mother's expertise,
I felt well dressed, sporting my made over clothes

The next few years were challenging times
With store bought clothes and the way they fit.
My rate of growth required large clothes --
Mother would say, "it's a little big, but he will grow into it.

A new shirt would be loose at the collar
And the seams at the shoulders pointed to the floor.
The sleeves at the wrists were always rolled back
And my hands would appear like opening a bureau drawer.

Mother's predictions were usually right on,
As to when a shirt would actually fit.
The problem, dear readers, as some of you experienced,
Was in a blink of an eye, I'd grow out of it.

My first Boy Scout shirt was something to see.
With its tucks and folds, beneath my hat, I resembled a tiny cloud -
But I carried our flag in the memorial parade,
And I know my folks were proud.

Time rolled on, in my growing years,
And I grew to be a conservative man.
I've often wondered if my being thrifty
Was part of my parent's plan.

TYKE

If ever I saw a gentle Giant
My Uncle Gilman would fill the bill.
Living "back in the woods", to him, was home,
One could say, "this was his will."

He had an easy laugh and a kind heart
That stood by him through thick and thin.
This is why, I'm reasonably sure,
The canine world was enamored with him.

A Sunday visit, with Uncle Gilman,
Was a real treat for me.
His dog would usually have a new trick,
Which was entertaining to see.

He named his dog, Tyke,
Because of her size.
She was just a little mongrel,
With big, blue eyes.

He rigged his doors so a little push
Would make them open and close,
This was handy for Tyke,
She could use her paw or nose.

Fetching a stick was easy for Tyke,
If it were thrown so that she could,
Tyke, however, did one better -
She went to the woodshed and,
One stick at a time,
Brought in the needed wood.

OWL FACE
(the catcher)

I was always a little intrigued
By the behavior of animals on our farm -
The way they responded to daily routine
Was certainly a touch of charm.

During the thirties and forties
We were diversified on our place.
Numbers weren't necessary for identification,
We could identify each animal by seeing its face.

There was a cacophony each end of the day
As daily chores took place.
Each animal, it seemed, had something to say,
Some were pitched high, others sang bass.

The water tub, in the barnyard, beckoned
As the cows eagerly quenched their thirst.
There was a little pushing and crowding,
To determine which would be first.

Once they were watered, civility reigned,
They no longer tried to race.
Once in the stable they knew where to go,
As each one went to her place.

Our horses were also part of the picture,
Each answered when its name was called.
They also knew just where to go -
Each one knew its own stall.

The cats came on the run
When their dish was rapped on the floor.
They knew that milk would be waiting
Next to the milk house door.

Owl Face was a little special,
She knew where there was more!
Once we started to milk by hand
She would follow along on the floor.

Every once in awhile I would take careful aim
To send a squirt in her direction.
She was a good catcher and seldom missed,
To the best of my recollection.

Owl Face was a clever cat,
Three colored with an owlish face.
Each year she presented us with a new family,
Her contribution, for controlling mice on the place.

13

THE BELL COW

I took a nostalgic walk the other day,
Some might call it down memory lane.
It's hard to say just why I did it --
There was nothing to lose and nothing to gain.

The path I followed was very familiar
'Though I hadn't traveled it for sixty years.
I envisioned my collie walking beside me,
With her tongue hanging out and flicking her ears.

Ahead, were the cows walking in line
Beating a path down to the gate.
A cow bell was ringing as they plodded along -
Then it was silent as they'd patiently wait.

I've heard it said that the bell cow was a leader
And that's the reason she wore the chime.
I can tell you, the bell cow wasn't a leader -
She was selected because she always lagged behind!

We usually had two bell cows
Although sometimes there were three.
It saved a lot of time hunting
Thus easier on a boy's legs, like me.

There were a hundred acres in our pasture
Including blackberry patches and more.
One could hunt 'til blue in the face,
It was a mighty tiresome chore.

On pleasant days, my dog herded
Them out of places too small for even a mouse.
If it started to rain and thunder,
Off she'd go as much to say -
"See you later boss, I'll be waiting down at the house."

Our Bell Cow was not a leader.

THE BIG ROOM

The teeterboards and swings are no longer there
And neither is the playground slide.
The fence is beginning to come apart.
The perils of time have been applied.

Tracks are noticeably absent
In the yard covered with snow.
It's where we played fox and geese,
During those years so long ago.

Names and faces come to mind
As I briefly stop for another look.
"Twas here I learned so many things
Not all of which came from a book.

Steam engines are no longer heard in the schoolhouse yard.
Large trucks seldom use route five.
The Interstate provides for bigger and faster
So this is where they drive.

As this noble edifice stands quietly, biding the passage of time,
There is hardly a way one could tell -
Of all its stories that could be told -
Now part of history and in the past they dwell.

Fifty-nine years have come and gone
Since I entered Mrs. Somerville's room.
Grades five through eight shared the "Big Room,"
Hence its nom de plume.

It was a status symbol, completing
Grades one through four in the "Primary room"
And advancing to grades five through eight in the "Grammar room."
We referred to them as the "little" and "big" rooms.

It was the fall of 1941 and the pangs
Of the depression had lingered on.
Little did we realize what lay ahead
And that peaceful thoughts would soon be gone.

Up until now, our recess conversations
Included our favorite radio programs such as
Tom Mix, Superman, Little Orphan Annie and more.
The bombing of Pearl Harbor was very sobering -
We were now involved in a war!

Most of us had older brothers and sisters
Who were called to serve their country's need.
Patriotism was running high and
Serving your country, was considered a noble deed.

New terms entered our conversations
Such as home front, victory gardens, defense
Stamps, rationing, black-out drills and more.
We practiced air raid drills, with a seriousness
We had never experienced before.

The Ralph Edwards radio program
Known as "Truth or Consequences," sponsored
A contest which was held nation wide.
The school that collected the most paper
Per pupil would host the program.
It was generally believed every school in the nation tried.

We had newspapers and magazines
Stacked to the ceiling in the school's basement and hall.
Win or lose we were giving it a shot,
"Answering our country's call."

Our next drive was collecting scrap metal
Which we piled on the school's front lawn.
Farm tools, junk cars, odds and ends -
Folks gave all they could, conservative times were gone.

Some of us served on the School Safety Patrol,
Though hardly a car ever went by.
Fuel was strictly rationed - two and a half
Gallons per week, for pleasure cars,
Was all that one could buy.

Mrs. Somerville saved her gas and each
Semester, treated those with perfect attendance,
To a movie and an ice cream sundae.
With an opportunity like this,
It was unthinkable to ever miss a day!

Of all my years in education,
A half century and more -
My fondest memories
Are those in the "Big Room,"
Completed during the war.

"Home Front"
World War II students of the "Big Room"
McIndoe Falls, VT Elementary School 1944

Front Row: Gordon Bogie, Raymond Somers, Frances Aiken,
        Jane Strew, Shirley Kendall
Second Row: Leslie Bogie, Jessie Sund, Priscilla Paye,
        Leslie (Bucky) Conant, Melvin Somers
Third Row: Ruby Cheney, Mary Helen Aiken, Carlton Crane,
        David Crane

18

EIGHT FOR A DIME PLUS A BOTTLE OF POP

In the fall of '41 I was selling the Saturday Evening Post
And some of my customers were all in a huff.
The price had increased from a nickel to a dime -
"Outrageous," some said, life was apparently tough.

I used to look forward to the next issue
To see what the cover would be.
A fellow by the name of Rockwell, did them
And they were most intriguing to me.

My commission was two and a half cents
For each magazine I managed to sell.
With only six customers one might conclude,
As a salesman, I wasn't doing that well.

Nevertheless, fifteen cents in a fellow's pocket
Was better than none at all.
It gave me a flash of independence
And a richly feeling of walking tall.

Not every week, but once-in-awhile,
I'd invite my younger brother to a tasty repast.
At Coburn's store we could get eight cookies for a dime and
A bottle of pop for a nickel (which we sipped to make it last).

Mrs. Coburn would furnish two glasses
As we sat at her table as big as you please.
Four cookies apiece and split the pop -
"Two country gentlemen," taking their ease.

A lot of water has gone over the dam,
Nostalgia is a feeling that refuses to stop.
Every now and then I think back to the days,
Of eight for a dime, plus a nickel for a pop.

COMPANY AT MILKING TIME
(Bonnie View Farm)

The mercury dipped below zero last night
And a bit of nostalgia came to mind.
Warm thoughts came into view
As I reminisced of a different time.

In '39 my Dad and I and the Hired Man,
Were milking twenty-four jerseys by hand.
On cold, winter nights the cow stable was
A cozy place, for both the beasts and man.

It was a farm-animal community
With each member in its place.
The dog, barn-cats, cows, calves, the bull-
All adding to the picture, with a certain touch of grace.

One could say 'twas a steady job -
Milking both morning and night,
But in retrospect, it was fulfilling,
And created a domestic sight.

By milking time the chores were done
Such as cleaning, watering and feed,
And one could almost feel the content,
As we fulfilled each animal's need.

On cold, winter nights, company came,
As we milked our cows by hand-
Some elderly fellows, living near by,
Each one a special man.

Percy would sit on an overturned keg
While Walt sat on a stool.
Don was a little restless and didn't sit,
But leaned on the wall, as a general rule.

20

They were all about my father's age
And had a great deal to say.
They would stay abreast as we proceeded with the milking,
Being extra careful to stay out of our way.

Each fellow lived alone
Which may explain why they stopped by -
But they enjoyed talking of yesteryear
And of what they had done in years gone by.

One had driven a six-horse hitch,
They all had cut corn by hand.
One had worked on the railroad -
Each one, to me, was a very, special man.

My memories are about all that's left of Bonnie View,
But crystal clear when the nights are cool -
And out in my barn, hanging on a nail,
Is my Dad's old milking stool.

DOUBLE CLUTCH IT

We had always depended on horses
To furnish our pulling power.
Then the day arrived when our Doodlebug came -
Truly the marvel of the hour!

Now the dictionary will tell you, in certain terms,
That a Doodlebug is a divining rod that is
Used to locate water, hiding beneath the ground.
To an eleven year old farm boy, however,
"It was the greatest machine that was ever found."

There were acres and acres that needed work,
To support the war effort and its noble cause.
What better excuse, for an eleven year old -
He could drive this rig without breaking the laws.

Having no muffler, it was a noisy rig,
But I didn't really mind.
For one reason, it quieted my shifting,
And muffled the transmission grind.

Although "I was ready" to solo
After a couple of minutes of advice -
My older brother suggested a check ride,
At least once or possibly twice -- or thrice.

So off we went with a jump and roar
As I ground the gears into their place.
He waved his hand and opened his mouth
And I knew I should stop, by the look on his face.

"Let me tell you something", he stated -
"This rig has four speeds ahead : low-low,
Low, second and high."
"If you don't Learn how to shift, you're going to
Break something and then you'll wonder why."

"The trick," he said, "is to double
clutch it when you shift and listen
To how the motor sounds."
"What you've been doing is grinding the
Gears and starting with leaps and bounds."

When he came home from the war in '45 the
Doodlebug was gone but we had a '38 truck.
I invited him for a ride, to watch me shift.
Thanks to his teaching, not a grind was struck.

Our 1938 Chevrolet truck.

FIVE, FIVE RING FOUR

Tempus fugit, as the saying goes,
It's amazing how time flies by.
Our footprints are recorded in the
Sands of time, as we climb
Life's mountains that reach the sky.

I find it hard to believe both are gone,
As well as their little store.
It seems as though I could pick up the phone,
And ask "Central" for five, five, ring four.

Clarice and Frank were very special
And extremely well liked by all.
Each year their grain store "came out" with free hats,
Making each of us kids stand tall.

If a stranger had passed by our elementary school
While recess was duly in session -
Seeing all the white hats might have caused him to think,
A wake was being held, or perhaps a special confession.

The McIndoes Cash Grain Store
Sold Wirthmore Feeds, also a little coal.
It would be considered small, by today's standards-
Back then it played a significant role.

Whenever we stopped to order our grain,
There was always a greeting at this little store.
Pleasantries were exchanged, the weather was
Discussed, and we talked about the war.

Grain was delivered in burlap bags,
Each one was carried by hand.
Sometimes Clarice would make the delivery --
She could lift them as well as a man.

As we "fed out" the grain we hung up the bags,
To protect them from dirt and grease.
Over a period of time, we returned them to the store -
They were worth a nickel apiece!

The railroad played an important role,
Bringing grain and coal to the store.
Steam engines would side-track the box cars
Of grain, special cars for coal - then
Continue their journey with supplies for the war.

A trait that made this couple special
Was a beautiful sight to see -
It was the time they took, talking to kids,
And listening to guys like me.

I know there are others with pleasant memories,
Much the same as mine.
We remember this couple with
A zest for life, to which they seemed to bind.

It's been said, "a man never stands taller,
When he stoops to help a boy."
If this is true, and I think it is, they never
Came taller than Frankie Strew, with
His philosophy of life that nothing could destroy.

A number of us are left, hunting and fishing,
The way he taught us to do -but more importantly,
Our philosophy of life was truly molded --
This, he taught us too.

Frank Strew, manager, and Mrs. Clarice Strew, bookkeeper.

McIndoes Cash Grain Store and warehouse.

AN HOUR'S NOONIN

My Dad was a hard working farmer
With certain principles to which he clung.
As I look back over sixty years,
He was my mentor, I was very young.

Although he was not a steady church goer,
To him, Sunday was a day of rest.
"You don't gain much by working on Sunday,"
I recall hearing him attest.

Being young and "wet behind the ears,"
I often charged into a job like a bull to a gate.
"Slow down," he'd say, "there's plenty of time,
You will last a lot longer at a moderate rate."

Whether we were splitting wood or digging potatoes,
He taught me neat little knacks:
Where to strike the chunk to make it split,
How to hold the potato claw, to save our backs.

Our noon day meal was a special time,
At least it was for Dad.
He enjoyed watching a fellow eat
And pondered a mite, as to what he had.

Although there was a heap to do
And little time to do it,
At least it seemed to me -
He insisted on taking an "hour's noonin"
Regardless of what others could see.

He believed it was important to rest awhile
After eating his noon-day meal.
It was time well spent, he always claimed,
Before heading back to the field.

Today, I see folks rushing here and there
With a cup of coffee in their hand.
I have to wonder if they'd be better off,
If an "hour's noonin," was part of their plan.

26

IT WILL, MORE'N LIKELY, SCOUR

Spring's work included the walking plow
As we "turned over" a new piece each year.
It was a time for a boy to get worms for fishing,
For apple tree leaves were the size of a mouse's ear.

As I searched for a worm can, Dad harnessed the horses,
They always furnished the power.
The plowshare was showing just a touch of rust,
But Dad said, "it will, more'n likely, scour."

So off we'd go across the piece,
Plowing a furrow in a straight, bee line.
With reins about his waist he steadied the plow,
As I, with my can, followed along behind.

At the end of the piece it seemed like magic,
The plowshare had blossomed like a flower!
The rust was gone, I had a few worms -
A little bit of effort, had caused the plow to scour.

An esoteric language seemed to develop
Between my Dad and me-
I'd ask him, at times, if something might scour
To which he'd reply, "we may have to wait and see."

At times I've wrestled with various problems,
Succeeding with some while others turned sour.
I've thought of my Dad and what he might say:
"With effort, it will more'n likely scour."

27

IT'S A SLIP, NOT A FALL

Mother was always there when I stubbed my toe,
A mishap that made a little guy bawl.
She had a way of soothing my feelings -
"It was only a slip, not a fall."

Medicated ointment and a roll of gauze bandage
Were always available with which she had a special knack.
I'm not really sure which was more soothing -
The homemade bandage, or Mother's pat on the back.

It was amazing, now that I think of it,
How problems would go away -
But a soft voice and a loving heart will
Move mountains, I've heard so many say.

Little folks have their troubles
And often it's hard to understand -
But one thing for certain, help is available
From a loving Mother, and her tender, helping hand.

From the time we built sand castles
And dreamed of castles built in the air -
Comfort was available if they fell apart,
Because a loving heart was always there.

"Set backs" are familiar in everyone's life,
Even those who appear to stand tall.
When one happens we need to resolve,
It was only a slip, not a fall.

IT'S GONNA BE A SCORCHA

As I strolled about the gounds of "Bonnie View,"
The temperature exceeded ninety degrees.
My mind went back to earlier times,
With days as hot as these.

Bunching hay and pitching on,
While hayseeds mixed with the sweat on my back,
Was one of my memories, as I strolled around,
Fending off tiny, black flies as they
Relentlessly mounted their vicious attack.

I thought of our horses, our faithful
Team, working up a lather as
They pulled our hay wagon with its large,
Wooden wheels - stamping their feet
And switching their tails, protesting the flies,
Letting us know just how it feels.

There was the long ride back on the
Load of hay, to continue with this little yarn,
Then pitching off and mowing back,
In a hot and dusty barn.

There was satisfaction, however,
As we backed the empty wagon outside.
To tell the truth, though sweaty and
Dusty, there was a certain touch of pride.

A mixture of oatmeal, sugar and
Water, quenched our thirst and
Helped to relieve this summer torture.
My Dad would wipe the sweat off
His face, then grin and say,
"I think it's gonna be a scorcha."

REFLECTIONS OF OL' JED

Ol' Jed was one of those special folks
One rarely gets to know.
Yet some would say, "he'd make your day,
As he swung his scythe both to and fro."

He could whet an edge, razor sharp
And cut a swath with an even stroke.
His work was done with a certain pride,
As attested by those with whom he spoke.

He was small in stature, but big of heart,
Standing less than five feet tall -
But had a way of making friends,
As folks stopped by to pay him a call.

He never seemed to be in a hurry
It was amazing how things got done.
His claim was, "planning your work and pacing yourself,
No need to go on the run."

"Folks are apt to bite off more'n they can chew,"
Was what Ol' Jed would say.
"There's just so much one can do
And so many hours in the day."

"If a place is gonna be kept up,
There's trimmin' to do and a little mowin' by hand."
"It's the little extras," according to Jed,
"That show a respect for the land."

As a boy, I didn't realize the depth of this man
Nor all of the values for which he stood -
But we can learn from others, through the pages of time -
If only we would.

Throughtout our years the fields of life need mowing
And some require a little mowin' by hand.
It's the extra trimmin' that really counts,
And precisely how we stand.

PILING WOOD (1935)

I remember my mother saying,
"It's hard to bake, using green wood."
There was a lot to do on East Hill
And though very young, I certainly understood.

With cows, horses, hens and pigs
Each waiting their turn to be fed -
Planning one's time was certainly required
And needless to say, looking ahead.

Cutting wood, with a crosscut saw,
Had to be done in the middle of the day.
Barn chores dictated the rest of the time-
As we headed home with a load on the dray.

The Dragsaw cut the logs into stove lengths -
It was then the splitting began.
Once it was split it had to be piled -
This was where my sister and I worked -
Doing the job of a man.

A five year old boy and a girl of twelve
Did a great deal on the family team.
Without computers, television, radio or
Electric lights, we got satisfaction,
By contributing to family esteem.

Once it was piled, we had a year to wait
For the wood to slowly dry.
We planned ahead each year
So mother wouldn't have to use green wood,
To bake us an apple pie.

THE LONG APPLE PEELING

Our apple orchard, of the 30's, was a choice spot
For a little guy like me.
It was made to order for a child's play
And provided a haven for the honeybee.

Sister Peggy would claim the yellow transparent
While I played under the peach -
But it was all in fun, as both of us knew,
There was plenty of room for each.

There were other apples such as
Dutch, and bethel, just to name a few.
The beehouse sat on the upper side,
Providing the honeybees an orchard view.

We classed our apples as early and winter,
A matter of family speech.
The bethel could be stored 'til late in the winter -
Early ones included the yellow transparent and peach.

The treats we had from this orchard
Formed memories deep in my mind.
It wasn't just the apples, dear reader,
But the hands that were gentle and kind.

The apple pies my mother made
Along with crisp and apple pandowdy,
Were enough for a little guy to grant high honors
And dub his Mom as summa cum laude!

Our Dad used to have a steady hand
As he peeled an apple for my brother and me.
We thought it might be the set of his chin,
Whatever it was, it was delightful to see.

The idea was to peel with a steady hand
And for us to watch and patiently wait.
We'd watch as the length of the peeling grew
And hold our breath for fear it would break.

If you toss a long peeling over your shoulder
It forms a letter as it strikes the floor.
The letter, of course, is supposed to remind you,
Of someone special, you secretly adore.

We'd watch as the length of the peeling grew
And hold our breath for fear it would break.

THE ONE HORSE COUNTRY STORE

Of all the memories I have of the past,
And they are numerous for sure -
One of my favorites that lingers on
Is the "one-horse country store."

One store keeper, usually the owner,
Was always ready to lend you a hand
The ones I knew were diversified folks,
Each one was a special man.

They knew each family and all its members
As they came by the store from time to time.
They also knew who needed help
And didn't have so much as a dime.

"Fred" had a family of ten to feed
Truly, a burdensome load.
But he came around whenever he could,
To pay a little more, on what he owed.

He would say, "Ben I'm a little, mite short
But I need a few things for the family to eat."
So Ben packed the groceries in a large box,
And threw in a little candy, for the children's treat.

Bert's store, in '38, was on its last legs.
It hadn't changed in forty years or so.
But a nickel bought a bag of chocolates
And for kids like me it was truly the place to go!

The store was a wonder for a small pair of eyes
There was so much for a kid to see.
Groceries and clothes were part of the list,
Also candy and ice cream for kids like me.

Five gallons for a dollar was the price of gas
But it had to be pumped by hand.
The storekeeper, with the white apron,
Was surely a diversified man.

There was a big, glass case with assorted candy
Ranging in price from a penny to a dime -
Licorice pipes, candy cigarettes and
Many others, "in step with the time."

Hoodsie ice cream cups were a special treat
And sold for five cents each.
With one cup and two spoons, my brother and I
Would head for the brook,"for an ice cream party at the beach!"

Pictures of movie stars on the cover of these cups
Kept us from tossing them away.
We could trade'em in for larger prints -
I still have mine today!

POOR MAN'S FERTILIZER

It's getting along into the month of April
Mack's Mountain is showing signs of spring.
Patches of snow are here and there -
Birds can be heard with the songs they sing.

Ice is out on Joe's Pond
Folks are beginning to rake their lawns.
Green grass is beginning to show -
Some might say, "winter is finally gone!"

Muddy roads are drying out
It's the end of the muddy season.
Winter tires are replaced by those of summer,
No sense in waiting, so many folks reason.

But then it strikes during the night
With a vicious anger and a whale of a blow -
And we wake up in the morning,
With half a foot of April snow.

As you talk to folks you get the notion
It's not as welcome as at Christmas time.
It's one more hurdle we have to clear
Or one more mountain we have to climb.

If we're inclined to look on the bright side of things,
We might consider what Dad used to say:
"It's a poor man's fertilizer
And good for an extra load of hay."

SHARING THE TUB

Taking a bath in the "dead of winter"
In the year of thirty-five,
Without central heating or electrical power,
One might wonder how you'd survive.

The oblong, copper boiler was placed on the kitchen stove
To heat the water for this weekly event.
The round, galvanized tub sat on the kitchen floor-
We considered it "heavenly sent."

With a large dipper in her hand,
Mother transferred the water from the boiler to the tub,
Then added cold water to make the temperature right.
Brother and I then gave it the "toe test" before
Climbing in to bathe on this weekly, Saturday night.

Efficiency was the word of the hour
As brother and I took our weekly scrub.
To save on water and the bar of soap,
We bathed together in this galvanized tub.

Though the wood-fired stove produced comfort
In the kitchen, it's about all that can be said.
For it was a long way to the kitchen chamber
And our beckoning feather bed.

In our pajamas, we headed upstairs
Followed by mother with a lamp in her hand.
Pleading then started to leave us the lamp,
Near our bed and on the night stand.

37

QUALITY TIME

The term, "quality time," is new to me
Though it's been around for quite some time.
The Great Depression and I started together,
When a penny was a penny and a dime was a dime.

Every now and again I reminisce
About how it was back then -
How we lived, what we did,
And whether or not we'd go through it again.

Although I don't recall using the term,
It appears "quality time" was rife.
Our family worked together and played together -
It was truly our way of life.

I spent many hours, hitching a ride
On the dump rake, as my mother
Drove our faithful team.
We talked about many things.
"Quality time," would it seem?

There were newly born calves
Puppies and kittens, truly life sublime;
Also rabbits and a flock of chickens.
Could this count as "quality time"?

Whether it was haying, cutting corn,
Or doing the milking by hand -
I was working and visiting with
My Dad, also with the hired man.

Getting ready for the Milk Inspector,
We all worked as a team.
It was important, of course, to ship our milk,
But also a matter of family esteem.

We spent evening hours fishing on the Connecticut river.
We deer hunted in the Fall.
There's something about family outings,
That make a person tall.

As I ponder today of yesteryear
I think it might be true -
We fit the bill for "quality time"
Because we always had something to do.

THE SPECIAL BUGGY RIDE

I took a little time, the other day,
To jot down some of my reflections --
Of childhood days and how it was --
To the best of my recollection.

Living on a farm, during the thirties,
Was a creative time, inventing all sorts of games.
There were scores of animals on the place,
All identified with special names.

It was a real treat, riding in a buggy,
Taking our eggs to Mr. White's store.
We traded our eggs for groceries--
Sometimes a little more.

He had a candy counter like you wouldn't believe -
It watered my mouth just to see.
Lollipops were a penny apiece -
Displayed of many colors, tempting little kids like me.

Holding my penny, tight in my hand,
I'd carefully survey this colorful sight.
A penny was hard to come by,
"So making a decision had to be right."

Once the trading was done, between Mr. White and Dad,
And the last word was said--
I made my usual lollipop decision--
Choosing the one that was bright, bright red.

Going home was three miles and all up hill,
A little tiring for the horse,
But that was okay, I had lots of time,
Licking my purchase, of course.

With conservative licks, as we headed home,
I could make it last with grace.
This included a stop to rest the horse,
By the waterbar, near Sam Thurston's place.

FRESH GREEN SHADES OF SPRING

As I look at Mack's Mountain from "Bonnie View Acres"
And ponder of all that the seasons bring -
I'm moved by the work of the Master's Hand:
"The fresh green shades of Spring."

From the light green shade of the aspen
To the dark green shade of the fir -
The shades of green are infinite in number.
It's that time of year when miracles occur.

New life seems to start at the mountain's base
And gradually ascend to the sky.
Each day of May brings forth more life,
Adding to the beauty for the observer's eye.

The new leaves unfurl with the innocence of youth
And appear to progress unafraid.
New life is born with patterns of the past,
Thus a bond with the old and the new is laid.

There'll be many trials, as the season wanes,
Many will be broken and torn -
But there's always hope in the ascension of growth,
Coupled with the time, when new life is born.

All of the seasons have their own beauty
And I'm grateful for all that they bring.
With new life, however, new hope is born -
Thus I welcome the fresh, green shades of Spring.

GRAMMIE'S HEART

Throughout the years, as time went by,
She nourished the children with heartfelt love -
Always ready, to dry their tears,
And share her thoughts, she was thinking of.

Doll's clothes were made by the score
With her able and willing hands -
And miniature roads, for little toy trucks,
Were constructed in the sand.

Girl Scouts and Boy Scouts were part of our Brood
And Grammie played a leadership role.
Camping, hiking and making friends -
She led, with all of her heart and soul.

There were basketball, soccer and hockey games
And Grammie was ready to go.
She was always ready to join in the cheers
While sitting and yelling near the front row.

The Grandchildren came, next in line.
It was a little like Deja Vu
But they all had their own little ways
And their love for Grammie too.

It was time for Grammie to go into action
And share her love with theirs.
With needle and thread and a little stuffing,
She soon created her special Bears.

Teddy Bears and Grandchildren
Go hand in hand -
At least it's what I've been told.
It helps a great deal, I truly believe,
If there's a Grammie with a heart of gold.

Our grandchildren are now grown
And perhaps enough has been said,
But I noticed, today, as I walked by the door -
A new batch of bears,
Residing on Grammie's spare bed.

I noticed, today, as I walked by the door-
A new batch of bears,
Residing on Grammie's spare bed.

I'VE SEEN THE OTHER SIDE

I've driven a number of second hand cars
Although a few were new.
I've worn a number of threadbare socks -
The ones your toes come peeking through.

When the toes came through the time had come,
The socks had reached a critical point.
It was time to change from one foot to the other,
So the toes and holes could each break joint.

Stories have been written about "rags to riches"
Describing some folks striking it rich.
I never wore rags or expensive clothes.
We were just about average, in our own little niche.

"Making do" is a character builder,
Though it may be foreign to some.
It's not with **what** we live, but **how** we live,
That determines what we become.

So many say, "it's not **what** you know,
But **who** you know that gets a person ahead."
This could be so, but a little mite risky -
Depending on ground where others tread.

There are times to keep our noses to the grindstone
And times to come up for air.
There are times we have to grit our teeth,
Carrying burdens too heavy to bear.

We'll take each day as it comes along
And adjust to each and every one -
But the cares of tomorrow will have to wait,
'Til the work of today is done.

THE HANDSHAKE

There's something about a handshake
That can add to a person's day.
It's a gesture that fosters friendship,
I've heard some people say.

A handshake, I've found, says a great deal -
Though a person may not utter a word.
It can tell you just how somebody feels -
A barometer, of sorts, so I've heard.

There are those who take your hand
While standing in a receiving line -
They'll smile a little then pull you along,
As though you were lagging behind.

There are others, however, who will grasp
Your hand and carefully pronounce your name.
With a friendly shake and a pretty, warm smile,
They let you know they're glad you came.

There's the death-grip shake that crunches your bones
And forces you down to your knees.
This usually comes with a slap on the back,
Which says, "you've never felt hands like these."

Then there's the limp, wetfish shake -
You pray the person won't cough.
One hesitates to shake this extended hand,
For fear it might fall off.

Some handshakes, 'I've received,
Made me wonder what the person had found.
For all the time he was shaking my hand,
His eyes were glued to the ground.

A firm, friendly handshake
With a smile in the eyes -
Tells you all you need to know
About making friends, and bonding friendly ties.

S.S.H.

45

THE HAT LADY'S BOOTH
(Kirby Quilters)

Two young ladies, with pretty long braids,
Stopped by a booth at the fair.
Though their stop was but a "flick of time,"
A gracious ambiance filled the air.

Their visit at the Hat Lady's booth
Was a touching scene to see.
A meeting of the minds of two generations,
Sharing their thoughts, is the way it looked to me.

I don't recall they spent a dime
Before they had to part -
But I truly believe, with their winning smiles,
They bought the Hat Lady's heart.

ICE FISHING

It's the middle of January,
The scene has changed on the Pond.
The camps are closed, the folks have left
And the boats are also gone.

Shanties have appeared, here and there,
With their various colors and size.
Some of them are truly a work of art,
Appearing as a fisherman's prize.

There are those who forego a shanty's comfort
And go forward with an auger and pole.
They sit for hours waiting for a bite,
Next to a little round hole.

One usually shifts, from time to time,
If the fish are slow to bite.
A number of reasons are usually given,
Before changing to a different site.

A big determinant in changing one's site
And moving to another stand,
Is the thickness of the ice, believe it or not,
And whether you bore by hand.

With a hand auger, on three feet of ice,
An assortment of tip-up poles -
One learns to pray that he will be lucky,
And find some ready drilled holes.

It's satisfying, however, going home with a catch
Knowing you've done your best -
But concerning when you offer a few to your neighbor
And he asks as to whether they're dressed.

KINELOPE AND ME

Some say I drive an antique truck -
I reckon it's an accurate claim.
Come fall foliage, she'll be twenty-six -
Kinelope, is her given name.

Three hundred miles per year is the usual limit
So neither of us really gets tired.
Since we work together in the summer only,
I suppose you could say, we're both duly retired.

I may be anthropomorphic,
But whenever the grandchildren arrive -
Kinelope's motor seems to purr like a kitten,
As we go on a hayride drive.

Kenelope's radio has an on and off button
Which also controls the sounds -
Thankfully, there're no automatic buttons
Such as bass, contralto, seek and find or whatever else abounds.

Her simplicity is very intriguing
As we travel down the road.
Each trip has a touch of nostalgia -
"Yesterday's faithful truck," carrying a modest load.

I've heard it said, when a fellow retires
He really needs lots of toys.
Not too different from his younger days,
He's still just one of the boys.

Keeping a farm truck, as well as a pickup,
Has to be rationalization personified -
But accepting retirement without a truck
Would be similar to accepting marriage without a Bride.

I often wave when I meet a fellow,
Driving his brand, new truck.
The payments must be rather substantial,
So I wish him lots of luck.

If you happen to meet an old Chevy truck
Being driven by an elderly man-
Be rest assured he's retired and happy,
And waving a friendly hand.

TOWN MEETING

Town Meeting is around the corner,
Folks have already started to talk.
Who's running for this and running for that?
Will the school bus run? Will some have to walk?

There will be those who favor a particular item
And those who will attempt to cast it asunder.
Sometimes it's hard, deciding who's right -
At least one has to wonder.

The meeting provides a chance to speak,
An opportunity to get things off one's mind.
Sharing a problem is excellent therapy-
Especially for those with an "axe to grind."

It's also a time to strengthen our friendship
With friends we hold so dear.
We have a proclivity of going our way,
Thus seeing some friends just once a year.

I've often thought I owe my Maker,
For a system so well defined.
We have our problems, but look around -
A better system, would be hard to find.

THE ELEVENTH DAY OF CHRISTMAS

Christmas and New Years came and went,
We've taken out our tree.
It "lit up" our lives for nearly a month
And was there for folks to see.

The ambience of a home is truly changed
When a tree is brought inside.
A touch of grace fills the air
While solemn thoughts abide.

It's time to move on, as the saying goes,
To a bright and joyous new year -
But we'll cling to some of our solemn thoughts
And our memories of those so dear.

NIGHT RAIDERS

Spring has arrived at Mack's Mountain
And it's not only the grass that's "riz."
Masked bandits are on their seasonal prowl,
To see just what there is.

Naps are over, appetites are heavy,
It's time to explore and discover.
Woe be to the trash cans, stored out back,
Especially those without a cover.

The bird feeders are cleaned each night
As though done by friendly elves.
Make no mistake, it's the night raiders' work
As they greedily help themselves.

With a mask on their faces, stripes on their tails
And a yen to prowl in the night -
One has to wonder about these bandits
That prefer to work without a light.

Along about August they'll add to their menu -
As we will discover by the light of morn.
I know not how they do it, but they seem to know
When it's time to raid our corn.

After all the complaints are said and done
There's really no reason for all the hype.
We have only ourselves to surely blame
For what little food these raiders swipe.

Later on there'll be some little 'ring tails"
Joining the picnic during the night.
They'll follow their parents to the "house of plenty"
Where an "honest" raider can find a bite.

All of a sudden a flash occurred
As bandits were busy in the night.
They were helping themselves to the birds' cuisine,
'Til someone turned on the light.

OLD JED'S THOUGHTS

I asked old Jed if it was cold enough for him
As the mercury hovered at 20 below.
He claimed he'd seen it a whole lot colder
Though just when it was, he didn't know.

He said he always listens to the weather report,
But gets a little baffled at how it's told.
"I don't really care," he went on to say,
"About fancy words, just tell me if it's gonna be cold."

Today it's the meteorologist talking about
El Nino and La Nina, confusing to an older chap.
I liked it when the weatherman said,
"You better bundle up, we're in for a long, cold snap."

We're told that global warming is melting the icebergs
And I'm sure they probably know.
They said this caused a warming winter,
But for a week now, it's been down to 20 below.

A lot of the ski areas complain
Because it doesn't snow when they think it should.
But, according to Jed, this isn't new.
He often used a wagon in January --
Would've used a sleigh, if he could.

Snow reports are often glum
And folks appear to be all in a sweat.
It doesn't always snow when we think it should
But, according to Jed, "winter ain't over yet!"

"It's ,more'n likely," according to Jed,
"We'll be getting our winter thaw."
"It probably won't come when we think it should -
Just one of those quirks about Mother Nature,
Or one of nature's predictable flaws."

Jed says, "we're all entitled to have our doubts,
The weather has always been anyone's guess-
But computers and satellites seem to help
And maybe they're something we need to address."

ONCE AGAIN

As March draws to a close
And the sun climbs higher in the sky -
The hardware stores are beckoning
With gardening tools to buy.

Daylight saving time is about to begin
Which means a head start for whatever we plan to do.
Mother's Day and Easter are around the corner.
Daffodils and tulips are peeking through.

Ice has long since been chipped from the walk,
The lawn is appearing as the snow recedes
I'm checking my tackle box for lures and line,
The necessities, if you please, of a fisherman's needs.

Garden seeds are lined up on the shelf,
Geraniums have been slipped and taking root.
Barring a drought, insects, weeds, blight and
Animals' appetites -- our garden will likely bear fruit.

I find it rewarding, this time of year,
To feed the birds and see the sun rise -
To see life renewed, once again,
Before the onslaught of little, black flies.

Ann E. (Watkins) Somers

PEACHAM'S SEASONAL SIDEWALKS

SEASONAL SIDEWALKS

The snowplows provide a dual service
As the roads in town are plowed.
The roads are opened for cars and trucks
And sidewalks are formed, for the peace-loving crowd.

They stretch for miles around the town
And beckon to those who like to stroll.
They offer fresh air and magnificent views -
Good for the body, soothing to the soul.

They follow the roads all around town -
No reason for one to get lost.
Homes are located along the way -
Ready to assist in adverse frost.

Roadside trees form green tunnels in summer
That turn color in autumn, white with the winters' snow.
The snow banks, however, provide seasonal sidewalks,
When the mercury drops down low.

There are certain requirements for traveling these paths,
It's up to the traveler to choose.
For a successful hike on these seasonal sidewalks,
One needs to select the right shoes.

Snowshoes, of course, are popular favorites,
Cross country skis are nice.
It depends, a lot, on the individual,
As well as the inevitable price.

These sidewalks are free from automobiles
And separate from the snow machine trails.
It's as though they were made for the peace loving hiker -
To enjoy winter's wonders, on a grandiose scale.

THE GRANDFATHER THEY ALL CALLED BUB

My Father-in-Law was a rare one
Who belonged, I think, to a special club.
When his grandchildren started walking and talking,
He encouraged them all to call him Bub.

The nickname caught on, over the years,
And never changed, to his dying day.
He was a kind and considerate man,
Liked by all, as I've heard so many say.

He was the kind of leader
Who led by a pull, rather than shove,
Thus making him special, in people's eyes,
And allowed him to bask in his Grandchildren's love.

An event occurred, one year, as the family
Gathered at Bub's and Grammie's place.
It could have been serious without proper action,
Bub outlined his plan with coolness and grace.

Bub's pigs had gotten loose from their pen
And proceeded to run rather free.
The Grandsons were eager to round them up
Which turned out to be a sight to see.

Each boy had an assignment to do,
Both the older and the small.
Pigs can be cantankerous at times
And not cooperative at all.

Instead of telling little Steve he was too small to help,
He gave him a safe job instead.
Bub placed him on a safe corner with a pail
And said, "if a pig comes by, throw this pail over his head."

The pigs were placed back in their pen
And everyone got in on the act.
No one was forced to be part of an audience,
Bub had seen to that.

58

AMBER WAVES OF GRAIN

As I drive by my neighbor's corn piece
From planting to harvesting time -
I'm often reminded of my youthful days
When I was eager and in my prime.

We used to plant four or five acres
Using a single row planter, pulled by a horse.
I used to lead ole Harry, my Dad steadied the rig -
Harry had a way of plodding along -
Creating "bent" rows, of course.

A neighbor stopped by one day
To pay us a visit and see how we'd been.
Our corn was up and he made a remark,
"I may have seen, more crooked rows,
But I can't remember when".

The corn piece was part of our vocabulary
From the first of June to early Fall:
"We got a good catch," knee high by the fourth"
And it stood over twelve feet tall.

Note was taken when it tasseled out
And when the ears appeared.
Will they ripen before first frost?
Was something we always feared.

As summer progresses,
I take mental note of my neighbor's corn.
Hundreds of acres, without a weed,
Clearly, a new age is born.

The sun was shining today,
As I drove by a large, flat plain.
The corn tassels swayed in a gentle breeze,
Like, "Amber Waves of Grain."

THE ICICLE

There's a March icicle growing at the corner of the house.
A late-winter wonder, under the sun.
It reveals the colors in the spectrum of light
And reminds me the sap is about ready to run

As time moves along there's less time to live,
Thus our lifetime gets shorter and shorter.
The icicle appears to have life in reverse -
As time goes by, it gets longer and longer.

There is no time for the icicle to think -
Indeed, it's absurd to believe that it does.
Far better, it is, to enjoy what we see,
Then to be concerned, about the way that it was.

While the icicle grows, so life moves along
And the deeds of busy folks are rife.
As the icicle reveals the spectrum of light,
Busy folks reveal the spectrum of life.

As this icicle grows at the corner of the house
Shedding drops of water, singing their song -
I'm comforted by knowing that others will follow,
Long after this icicle is gone.

It's been most pleasant, though only a short time.
Observing this icicle in all kinds of weather -
Though our lives are different, thery're symbolically the same,
I feel most fortunate, we've spent time together.

The icicle has taught me the colors of light,
The way life is and will always be -
To accept each day as it comes along,
And help make the World a better place to be.

FLOYD 1999
(Did he do more good than harm?)

Our spring had gone dry for the first time
In a decade of plentiful years.
The plants in the garden had a withering look
And a poor yield was one of our deepest fears.

As the summer proceeded with its sun drenched days
Providing vacations to remember -
A price was being paid by the flora world,
From the first of June until early September.

The rivers and streams had a moribund look,
Fish were easy prey for the otter.
Springs and wells were going dry -
Folks were getting desperate for water.

Drawing water is not much fun,
Especially if you live on a farm.
The animals, it seems, always drink more,
Thus diminishing the barn chores' charm.

How many are grateful for a drink of water
Or a chance to wash the car?
A little water, if you please, to brush your teeth -
A convenience for anyone, regardless of whom you are.

It's interesting, even amazing,
How we live from day to day.
We're inclined to take many things for granted,
Until fate tips his hand
And forcefully "demands his pay."

When Floyd came, all we heard
Was the damage that he might bring.
It was rare, indeed, to hear some say
Just what he'd do for our spring!

We were out of power for a few days,
A fact we readily admit.
But our spring is now on a "watery mend,"
Thanks to Floyd and his "drenching hit."

There are those who would say,
"It might have been better without the force of a bull!"
All we can say is you're probably right,
But the choice, it seems, was neither a push nor a pull.

There's a certain mystique about tropical storms
Regardless of their obvious fault,
Just how do they gather moisture from the ocean
And how do they extract the salt?

Though a price was paid for the actions of Floyd
As he proceeded north on his windy cruise,
He ended the drought without a doubt
And thereby paid, his tempestuous dues.

GOOD MEDICINE

We sometimes wonder how we project
And how people will speak on our behalf.
One of the kindest comments folks could say about me,
Is, "that fellow really knows how to laugh."

Some folks, I've noticed, utter little, light laughs
That remind me of tiny ripples, dancing on a pond -
But the laughs I enjoy, tickle your belly,
The ones folks remember, long after you're gone.

There're laughs, of course, that cover hurt feelings
While one projects a brave, new face.
The lips are sending a few cross signals
And the stomach is churning at a rapid pace.

There're also little, light titters, some people use,
Especially if they're not sure what to say.
They seem eager to enter a conversation,
But aren't quite sure just how to play.

I've noticed a few who seem a little nervous -
While talking, they twist and they wiggle.
They don't appear to enjoy what they're doing,
And attempt to cover with a nervous, little giggle.

Then there are those with a loud guffaw
Which usually comes in with every other word.
I question if they have that much to say -
But it's important for them to always be heard.

A hearty laugh is real, good therapy,
It's also contagious with those you're around.
What a gift it is to exchange with others,
This wonderful feeling, this magical sound.

There are some who will say a glass is half empty,
While others will say it's half full.
The difference between negative and positive thinking,
Is like moving a string with a push or a pull.

The message, I think, to unhappy people,
If I may speak on their behalf -
Is don't stick around negative folks,
But surround yourself with those who laugh.

64

COURAGE AND FAITH

The congregation was singing a familiar hymn,
"Love Devine, All Loves Excelling."
I stopped singing, for what I saw
Touched me deeply- was most compelling.

The choir was descending from the loft
To sit with the folks in this grand, old church.
It was time to listen to another message -
Time to ponder and our souls to search.

Six or eight steps lead to the loft,
Really, not an arduous task-
Not, that is, if your body is strong,
Otherwise, there're questions one might ask.

With a magnifying glass suspended from her neck,
A brace on her ankle and a cane in her hand -
This brave little lady led the choir from the loft,
With courage and faith that seemed so grand!

She descended the steps with a cane in one hand, the other on the rail,
Her hymnal was waiting in the pew.
She had memorized the hymn, or at least the first verse -
It was all so subtle and matter-of-fact,
I wonder, how many knew.

There are tears of sadness and tears of joy
Also, of admiration, I've heard some say.
I stopped singing for tears of admiration-
This little lady, did something for my day.

I'm growing old and my eyesight is dim -
But after watching this lady step down from the loft,
My courage and faith have been reinforced,
I'll climb life's stairs to our Maker's Loft.

THE SCYTHE IN A TREE

The land has a gentle slope
From the old town road down to the outlet of Foster Pond.
There are cellar holes here and there,
Remnants of homes, of the people long since gone.

Trees have grown up and hidden the land
And obstructed a magnificent view.
One needs only to look at the surrounding mountains,
To imagine the beauty those folks once knew

Ced and I had come to this place
To hunt grouse and enjoy the autumn air.
We were slowly walking, to stalk our prey,
When we came upon something that shouldn't be there.

We noticed the ground had become a mite softer
As we proceeded down the sloping land.
Indeed, it was just a bit swampy,
Barely supporting the weight of a man.

These conditions created an ambience
That seemed to explain what we were about to see.
It was truly a piece of history
That amazed both Ced and me.

There before us was a large cedar tree
With a scythe protruding therefrom.
Over a hundred years had come and gone
As this tree grew and waited,
For the owner to come.

Since the soil was too soft for horses
There had been no choice for this man.
He did what others always did --
"Mowed this chunk by hand."

But why did he hang his scythe on a branch
And leave it for a hundred years?
The snath had rotted off and fallen to the ground
Leaving the scythe in a cedar bier.

It's more than likely, we will never know
Who owned this scythe or where he went,
But he left a visual, piece of history
And perhaps that's the way, this story was meant.

67

LIFE

There are certain burdens we have to bear -
Not everyone carries the same size load.
This might be the reason, why you and I,
Don't always walk down the same, narrow road.

There are times when all of us have our doubts,
And the winds of life blow bitter tones.
We hesitate to walk on certain roads,
For fear of tripping, on all the stones.

Accidents appear to be inevitable,
We're bound to stub our toe -
But each time we learn a little bit more -
This, perhaps, is the way we were meant to grow.

There are shortcuts available. if we're willing to listen
And take heed of experiences of others.
We can learn of the pitfalls of those before us
And share the knowledge with our sisters and brothers.

Two millennia have come and gone since
The Teacher of teachers taught a new lifestyle:
If forced to walk a bitter road,
Offer to walk, an extra mile.

MEL'S LIBRARY THOUGHTS

Our library has many doors,
Ready for opening to here and there.
The beauty is where you can go,
Without ever leaving your chair.

Guides are provided, if you wish to travel,
And highlights are held in your hand.
Trips may be carefully outlined,
For travel in distant lands.

If research is your beck and call
And there's an item you wish to explore,
Our library stands ready to lend a hand
And provides a special door.

As I take my stand with older folks
And ponder as to where and when,
I find myself by a library door,
That highlights where I've been.

Experience is a good teacher
But surely has its flaws.
Without a guide we sometimes fail
And never know the cause.

It's paramount, as time goes by,
As surely as the lion roars -
To befriend young and old to our library,
With all of its friendly doors.

SIGNS OF SPRING AT BONNIE VIEW

It's late winter, 2003 and
I'm beginning to look for a few signs of spring.
Water is dripping from the eves on the house,
On the roof, patches of snow stubbornly cling.

Birch trees have straightened their winter stance
After shedding their winter's load.
Sugar Makers are beginning to stir
And think of "breaking" their sugaring roads.

We've had plenty of the "white stuff" at Bonnie View,
But I'm sure we'll get some more -
Finding a place to put it all
Is a familiar, late winter's chore.

Our winter, feathered friends patiently wait
As I refill their feeding trays.
Sharing with summer, feathered friends
Is around the corner,
But I doubt if they're counting the days.

Our potato bin is beginning to show signs
That eliminate all reasonable doubts -
As each potato heralds the coming of spring,
By producing a new set of sprouts.

Our dirt roads at Bonnie View are frozen,
But the snow banks have a rotted look.
When they disappear we'll not complain,
But ponder on how long it took.

Starting the tomatoes is an early, seasonal chore,
One we cherish each Spring.
It's not just planting for future food,
But enjoying the grace, that new plants bring.

After said and done and thinking it through,
We're grateful at Bonnie View.
Each season offers a touch of grace,
As well as something new.

SUGAR ON SNOW PARTY

Mrs. Higgins, from down country,
Arrived in our home town.
It was sugaring time, the trees were tapped,
The farmers were scurrying around.

The big event, for this time of year,
Held in the Village, Town Hall -
Was the sugar on snow party,
A popular event, one enjoyed by all.

To make this party a real success,
It had to be planned just so.
There was silverware on the tables
And aluminum plates, and people sat toe to toe.

To the novice, now, like Mrs. Higgins,
Let me set your mind at rest -
Sugar on snow is really syrup on snow,
And eating it, can be a real test.

The procedure for serving, at a party like this,
Is to pile some snow on everyone's plate-
When this is done and everyone's served -
The syrup is served, at a rather brisk rate.

Now Mrs. Higgins didn't know all of this -
The procedure wasn't mentioned, where she sat.
So when they served her a plate of snow, she exclaimed,
"Oh I can't eat all of that!"

SPECIAL GLUE FOR SOLID BONDS

Of all the riches there are in this world,
There is only one for Ann and I.
It's neither money nor property that catches our fancy,
It's the love that shows in our children's eyes.

We've had our share of "up hill sledding,"
As the family matured and grew.
Each situation was a new experience for living and learning,
From which each member drew.

From our family's early age to later years,
Each member had to do and go beyond.
It might be said, as an after thought,
"It took a lot of glue to form a bond."

As we tried to adjust to meet new changes,
Questions arose from time to time.
It became eminently clear, at an early age,
There were mountains we would have to climb.

We eventually learned that to understand, we needed to listen,
To use good reason, we needed to share.
A shared problem could be lightly borne,
Without this sharing, it was too heavy to bear.

As the years passed by, maturity grew -
Not only in the children, but in Mom and Dad.
We now had teenagers with experienced parents -
Or a little more experience than they had.

Educational choices had to be made
As preparations were made for a changing world.
There were hesitations and hidden fears.
Are we ready? Are we good enough? Should we give it a whirl?

Leaving the nest, to build their own,
Was the biggest step of all.
Parents may suggest, but they don't decide,
They pray that each will stand proud and tall.

The grandchildren arrived one by one,
As a new generation began to dawn.
In retrospect it seems apparent,
"It was special glue, that formed a solid bond,"

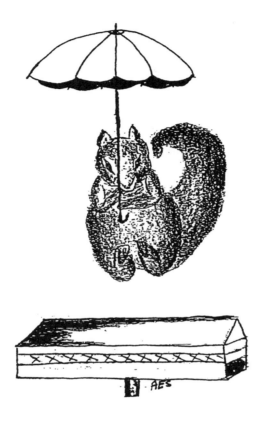

Though the food is laid out for my feathered friends
That can be reached only from the air -
These acrobats have a calculating eye
And, an uncanny will to grab their share.

BACKYARD ACROBATS

They perform in the winter as well as the summer,
Also in the fall and spring.
They give the impression that life is a party
And eating is a year around fling.

Though the food is laid out for my feathered friends
That can be reached only from the air -
These acrobats have a calculating eye
And, an uncanny will to grab their share.

With their four little paws, more like hands,
It's amazing how they swing through the air -
And once they've landed where the food is placed,
They go into a stance as though in prayer.

The way they can climb up a metal pole
And slide down to a feeder, hung by a string,
Makes me believe they're really saying -
"Who needs feathers or a floppy wing?"

As I go out each morning to feed the birds,
In winter, the snow is above my knees.
This is no problem for these acrobats -
They've developed little snowshoes, if you please.

They sail through the air with the greatest of ease
And jump high objects with a single bound,
Hang high in the air with just one paw
And snitch the bird seed, if there's any around.

As I watch this performance day after day,
I'm convinced I've truly been fleeced.
These little guys, with their furry tails,
Are using my yard for a daily feast.

I continually invent new ways of winning,
To hold these guys at bay -
But the more I dream of winning this contest,
I hereby submit -- so do they.

THE TEACHER

A good teacher is God's gift to children,
One whose work is never done.
Always ready with a helping hand -
And finding ways to make learning fun.

There's a special knack, working with folks,
That's truly rare under the sun.
Being willing and able to identify -
And making each feel, like they're the only one.

A good teacher is deeply committed
To all hours of the day -
Teaching and leading by personal example-
Knowing students learn more by what you
Do than whatever one might say.

Leaving home for school, for the first time,
And letting go of Mother's hand -
Is disconcerting to say the least,
Thank God for the teacher who will understand.

It's heart warming to see little folks read -
With a touch of "magic" they've been encouraged to try.
It's beautiful to see the teacher's pride,
As a tiny tear appears in her eye.

Mrs. Harvie and her
Kindergarten Class

Note:
   Mrs. Harvie was named "Teacher of the Year" by her Supervisory District in Barre City, Vermont in the year 2004.

TURNING WATER

Spring came a little mite early and
El Nino is to blame, according to some.
Whatever it was, we shouldn't be fooled -
More cold weather is likely to come.

Sap buckets are being hung.
Water is running from the melting snow.
Frost heaves and ruts are with us again -
Also the mud -- wouldn't you know ?

Each spring there's a quantity of water
That rampantly and freely flows.
Like a lot of us, it needs a little help,
In determining the direction it goes.

It's a time when culverts seem destined to plug,
Just when they're needed the most.
It's also a time to truck a little stone -
But the soft roads say, "it's time to post"

We had water bars before culverts
And I'd say they had their place.
They made good trigs to rest a horse,
But made it rough if you cared to race.

In the summer, the water bars tested
A hay maker's skill.
Going over these humps with a poorly built load,
Would nearly guarantee a hay maker's spill.

Instead of plowing the drive and shoveling the walk,
There's water we have to turn.
It's not a bad change and there're no black flies,
Or a hot, summer sun that's ready to burn.

The crocuses and daffodils will soon be up,
Making their triumphant return.
Meanwhile, we go with first things first -
Right now, there's water we have to turn.

BYWORDS ?

I'm inclined to agree with a saying I've heard,
"The more things change the more they stay the same."
What you hear, often times, is not really new
But a different twist, by those we're apt to blame.

It used to be, if a fellow was "SQUARE" he
Was one you could always trust.
Regardless of what others said or did,
Here was a person, right and just.

WOW, is a word that was often used
But in time, was replaced by SWELL!
Each generation needs a new identity -
"The old expressions no longer gel."

TERRIFIC, also had "its day in court,"
But was eventually replaced by GREAT!
Once again, we took a new turn -
Brand new folks with a brand new slate.

SUPER, was around for a year or so
Then came RADICAL, long and strong.
Folks were singing with brand new words,
But what they were singing was the same old song.

AWESOME, made its debut not long ago,
Adding one more expression to the esoteric pool.
It was, alas, to be replaced -
In the minds of some, "it's no longer COOL."

CHOOSE YOUR RUTS CAREFULLY

Spring has sprung on Mack's Mountain,
Spawning thoughts of yesteryear.
Our horses and wagons have long since gone,
But memories linger, ever so dear.

Mollie and Nellie, dapple gray mares,
Were always willing and strong of heart.
They needed no urging, in knee deep mud,
To pull the load on a large wheel cart.

As the season progressed, drying the mud,
Ruts appeared where the mud had been.
Traveling from here to there, on a rutty road,
Required patience, prayers and a Grand Amen!

Outsiders spoke of a year's four seasons:
Winter, Spring, Summer and Fall -
But we always claimed a fifth --
Mud season was the one that stood tall.

Although our horses are gone,
Mud season continues to be.
It seems to say, "before you have summer,
You have to put up with me."

Mud season reminds us of a way of life
With all of its pits and trials -
"Choose your ruts carefully,
You'll be with'em for a number of miles."

ONLY SCRAP REMAINS

As I stop to ponder of what remains,
There is very little for folks to see.
What once was a "going concern,"
Is now but a memory to me.

Like so many other small farms of the thirties,
We were diversified, as some would say.
Haying in the summer, cutting wood in the winter,
Milking by hand, each end of the day.

Repairs on the buildings were continuous,
There seemed to be no end.
We would no more'n get one job completed,
When we'd find something else to mend.

I don't recall anyone counting the hours
That each one worked per day.
The work was there and had to be done -
It seemed like the only way.

Seventy-three years have come and gone
Since the period of which I speak.
I haven't drawn a complete picture,
But at least you've had a peek.

Not long ago I visited the site
Where our sugar house used to be.
T'was once a "going concern,"
Is now but a memory to me.

There's a touch of excitement that seems to abide -
A change in routine, from long, winter's chores.

SUGARIN
IN MY NECK OF THE WOODS

The "sweet season" is raising it's head
And talk around town has a special flair.
It's hard to say what brings it on -
There are those who think it's a change in the air.

The sugar house shed is full of wood,
Cut and piled the year before.
Roads are broken through the sugar place,
Just part of the sugarin chore.

Town meeting is around the corner
And it's certainly a foregone bet -
Sideline talk will be taxes and roads
And whether anyone has tapped yet.

At local stores, Post Office and Town Clerk,
Rumor has it that somebody has boiled,
But it's not clear how much was made,
Nor specifically, what its grade.

It's usually not long, after the first report,
Before steam is escaping from sugar house doors.
There's a touch of excitement that seems to abide -
A change in routine, from long, winter's chores.

As the season progresses and snow disappears,
Spring makes its annual mark.
The roads get muddy, the sap slows down,
And the last of the run gets dark.

The job ahead creates mixed feelings,
Admittedly, not as much fun -
Cleaning the equipment and putting it away -
This sugarin season is done.

SUCCOTASH ROWS

The older we get the more memories we have
As the days fly by, one by one.
A blessing, however, is the time we have
For choice recollections, before each day is done.

There were birthday parties for each of the children
As they grew older and taller each year.
Milk and cookies were laid out for Santa,
As we bulged at the seams with holiday cheer.

Tricycles, bicycles, little toy trucks -
Dolls, teddybears, a dog and a cat,
Rabbits and guinea pigs to name a few.
Oh yes, we also had two white rats.

On camping trips we learned about nature,
Such as singing frogs and fish in schools.
It seemed that nature wasn't fair to frogs
Because only the toads were provided with stools.

As baby rabbits, kittens and puppies arrived
They each, of course, were given a name.
Nature study was to continue -
Trying to determine from whence they came.

"Helping hands" is one of my favorites,
As we prepared our garden one spring.
We talked of how our seeds would grow
And of all the nice things they'd bring.

Unbeknown to us, little hands intervened
And mixed the seeds altogether.
Sorting them out was out of the question -
Like trying to comb the parts of a feather.

Back then, money was tight and budgets were limited,
A fact that most everyone knows -
So we planted this potpourri of garden seeds
And raised a garden with succotash rows.

A RIDE ON THE CRUST

I went for a nostalgic walk this morning -
It was only a notion, but seemed like an absolute must.
A late, winter thaw had provided the setting,
As I strolled around on the crust.

So many memories came to mind
As I looked around at the grounds.
I could picture my childhood friends sliding,
And could almost hear the sounds.

Sliding on the crust was quite an affair,
Involving all of the kids in town.
Once the crust was tested and found to be adequate,
It was amazing how the word got around.

We even took our sleds to school --
Quite a sight to see, when all lined up outside.
If we hurried real fast, at recess time,
We could usually get in a second ride.

There was a hill in back of the school
That sloped upward to a neighbor's farm.
As I picture all of us sliding down this hill,
It's a tender memory, with a certain, magical charm.

Flexible Flyer, Speedaway, Flying Arrow and Red Diamond
Were some of the brands, each used with a touch of pride.
Others were homemade with special features,
Such as wider runners, to give you a "smoother" ride.

As I finished my stroll, back to the house,
I felt an impulse, a little like an inward thrust.
My homemade sled, that hangs in the barn -
Beckoned, for one more ride on the crust.

SAWING WOOD WITH THE OL' ONE LUNGER
1930 AND 40'S

Winter, barn chores took most of the day,
But there was wood to be cut, if we were able.
There were usually a few hours, in the middle of the day,
When we could "break loose" from the stable.

We would harness up Chubby and Harry
And hitch'em up to the dray -
Then head for the woodlot with ax and crosscut saw,
Getting one more load, day after day.

We cut the wood to "handling length"
Which varied from six to eight or ten feet -
Piled it on the dray and headed home,
With two wet mittens and two cold feet.

As the winter progressed, our woodpile grew
And finally the time would come -
We now had to cut it to "stove length,"
Meaning the circular saw and One-Lunger,
Had to be lined up and plumb.

The One Lunger was a heavy old brute
Mounted on skids, requiring the horses
To "snake" it around.
She needed priming and pampering
To get her started - first a putt, putt
And then a wheezing sound.

Once she was lined up with the
Circular saw and the big, leather
Belt was in place -
We were ready to saw "stove length" wood,
With a lot of noise and a touch of grace.

My Dad ran the table, I threw
Away, the hired man "handed on."
Danger lurked just inches away
And the screeching sound was hard on the ears.
The days, of course, have long since gone,
But fond memories have lingered, throughout
The years.

LET'S HEAR IT FOR THE U.S. MAIL

Throughout the year we get lots of mail -
Most of it gets thrown away.
Just how our address gets "spread around,"
I'm sure I couldn't say.

There're always bills near the end of the month
As regular as the morning sun.
We pay what we can and hope for the best,
Before the month is done.

Sweepstake letters are always coming,
Telling how rich we just might be.
"No purchase required," they always say,
And a stamp is your only fee.

Animal shelters always need money
And it's hard to pass them by.
They send a picture of the cutest pets
That wrenches your heart and moistens your eye.

Institutions ask for financial support,
A most worthy cause I would agree.
I feel as though I should help what I can
Because a number of folks helped me.

Friends remember my special day
When I can "blow my personal horn."
They send me cards and wish me well,
To celebrate the day I was born.

There's a mid-winter day that warms the heart
And brightens the sky above.
It's Valentine's Day and a card appears,
Expressing one's heartfelt love.

Yuletide, however, brings out our best,
And I've never known it to fail,
It's when we hear from family and friends -
With a bountiful supply of Christmas mail.

TRADING CARS

Trading cars is serious business,
At least it is to me.
One can't afford to be too eager,
I'm sure most folks would agree.

A few days ago we went shopping
For a car that would meet our needs.
Nothing special, you understand,
Just a practical car, my wife and I agreed.

As we drove into the autoyard, there
Were cars as far as one could see -
And in every window of the sales building
Stood a salesman, as though on a ship at sea.

We had no more than got out of our car
And started to look around,
When a salesman was standing by our side
Expounding the good points of every car -
Similar to a clock, that's been tightly wound.

In order to create a subtle air
We allowed we were just looking around-
To get an idea of prices to compare
And what was available in town.

We had our eye on a particular car,
But tried not to let it show.
After asking a few questions we moved along
But I'm sure he had to know.

After walking in circles and looking back,
We knew our guard was down.
A few more questions, he handed us the keys
And invited us to drive it around.

The next move was to announce the price
And make it a plausible sound.
After using his notepad and juggling some figures,
His eyebrows arched like a Basset Hound.

The price, of course, sounded high
And we asked if that was the best he could do.
"Not really," he said, "call me tomorrow
And we'll do our best by you."

Tomorrow came, the price was down,
But still was up too far.
So we offered to "split the difference"
But he suggested we buy a cheaper car.

We knew the car we really wanted
And so, alas, did he.
I looked at my wife, she nodded her head
And that was enough for me.

After buying the car and heading home,
A little like soldiers in full retreat,
We got the car we really wanted,
But had to wonder, how much we got beat.

TRYING YEARS

Teenage people are at a frustrating time,
They want so desperately to fly.
They're experiencing all kinds of new-felt moods,
And don't always know just why.

It's seldom easy to explain to their folks
Exactly how they feel.
Feelings, sometimes, are easily hurt
And it seems, at times, that they never will heal.

We try so hard to make it clear
That it's a period we all go through.
This only "pays part of the bill,"
Because to them, it's an experience that's new.

Parents attempt to draw parallels between
Teenagers lives and that of their very own.
Some of this helps because it's true,
But some of it gets lost with a discordant tone.

It's a transition between the freedom of
A young child's selection of play,
And the responsibility of a young adult
Organizing and planning, to get the most of each day.

Surely, it's a time for a certain amount
Of freedom, and time to have some fun.
It's also time for a certain amount of reason -
Determining, a little, how things get done.

Restricting as it seems, during these trying years,
It's a loving parent who insists on reason.
Responsibility and discipline are not meant to hurt,
But to make a solid person to cope with the season.

WHAT MAKES FEBRUARY SPECIAL

At my age, every month is special if I'm still around to see it and my
Health is reasonably sound --
But February is extra special, when you weigh it against the others
And compare them pound for pound.

It's the month of Washington's and Lincoln's birthday -
William Henry Harrison's too.
If you look to the North on a sunny day,
You will notice the sky is an extra brilliant blue.

The sun is climbing higher in the sky,
Folks start thinking of spring.
Sap will soon be running,
Even the birds are beginning to sing.

We look for the sleeping Ground Hog
To wake up on the second day.
We don't really think we'll see him,
But then again, we may.

Seed catalogs are arriving in the mail and
We have to start thinking about sprouting potatoes.
Around Washington's birthday, some folks believe,
It's time to start the tomatoes.

There are numerous holidays being celebrated
Here and around the world.
Each one, it seems, is especially designed
For a certain group, a boy or a girl.

In February, however, there's a special day
That's understood by all mankind.
It's a day that reminds us of thoughts from the heart -
Being charitable to others, placing our troubles behind.
Won't you be my valentine?

WOODEN WHEELS WITH IRON TIRES

Buggies, express wagons, hay wagons, lumber wagons
And two wheeled gigs used to travel the street in my home town.
They were some of the last of years gone by,
The end of an era was winding down.

They all had one thing in common,
Something that was gracious to see-
Wooden wheels with iron tires,
Drawn by horses, often driven by boys like me.

My first play wagon, handed down from Grandmother,
Was truly a prize to admire!
It was fashioned, a great deal, like the "real" wagons,
And traveled on four wooden wheels,
Each, with an iron tire.

Horace drove a light trotting horse
That went with a noticeable "hitch",
Or perhaps it was more like a limp,
I really can't tell you which.

At any rate, he always went on the trot,
Exemplifying a strong will and determined pluck,
As Horace rode in his express wagon-
A horse-drawn forerunner, of the modern pick-up truck.

Leon drove a pair of medium sized horses
They probably weighed about 900 each.
I would wave to him as he made his daily treks
On a lumber wagon, without the body -
He and his dinner pail, rode on the reach.

As he slowly passed by, his head bent down,
There was not even a hint of emotion.
The horses feet just plodded along-
One had to look twice to detect any motion.

We were farming with horses, at the time,
And they required attention on each end of the day.
They had to be cleaned, bedded,
Watered and carded, as well as brushed,
And given an ample amount of hay.

A boy, back then, learned to drive at an early age
With a pair of reins in his hand.
Wagon jacks and greasing wheel axles,
Were routine for a growing, little man.

If a wheel broke or a tire fell off,
We took it to Fent's Mill for repair.
He could replace the spokes, hubs or tires-
It was comforting to know he was there.

The memories have grown fonder as time goes by
And I think of the future and what may transpire,
But I truly saw an end to the era,
Of wooden wheels with iron tires.

Wooden wheel with an iron tire

WRAPPING GIFTS
FOR MY QUEEN

Christmas is but a day away;
The gifts are under the tree.
Pretty ones were wrapped by you know who,
The others were wrapped by me.

I've watched many times, year after year,
As her hands and scissors work in tune.
The paper responds to her magic touch
As though she was spinning a cocoon.

I use paper from the very, same batch,
Plus scads and scads of scotch tape.
One would think I had an inborn fear,
That the gift inside, was trying to escape.

I have a reverent feeling to the genius
Who invented stick-on bows.
They add a lot of color, a little touch of class,
And rescue me from my wrapping woes.

After wrapping the gifts with my clumsy hands,
I strategically place them under the tree -
Tape on the back, folds on the bottom,
A stick-on bow for all to see.

As I present my gifts to the one I love,
The tape, is on the back side.
Though my hands are clumsy at wrapping gifts,
They are tender, toward what's inside.

FRIENDS

How rich I feel, as time goes on,
To have so many friends,
And what a privilege it is to count them -
As each year so nobly ends.

FRIENDS

How many times, during our lives,
Do we stop to count our friends?
The ones who are there to soothe the soul
And offer a "hand" for your heart to cleanse.

We've often heard we should count our blessings
But this usually falls on doubtful ears.
It's a little like whistling in the dark,
To mask our hidden fears.

We seem to have a proclivity
Or perhaps I should say, a knack -
Of worrying about some who appear to be walking,
On the other side of the track.

Instead of worrying about the other side,
Might it be better to offer your hand?
It just might be, therapy for both -
Helping one another to understand.

Near the end of the Civil War Abe
Lincoln was asked, "how will you punish
Our enemies and make them pay amends?"
Abe replied, "I'll destroy all of my enemies,
By making them all my friends."

How rich I feel, as time goes on,
To have so many friends,
And what a privilege it is to count them -
As each year so nobly ends.

WHAT MAKES A SPECIAL FRIEND

What makes a special friend
And what makes that friendship grow?
Is it a quality that one can measure?
Does anyone really know?

How long does it take for a friendship to grow?
And how do you know, when it's fully grown?
Though it may be elusive to quantify,
The final product, is very well known.

Thinking about my closest friends
Is a warm and loving thought
And through the years I've been enriched
By all the warmth it's brought.

There are times when all of us have our doubts,
And the winds of life blow bitter tones.
We hesitate to walk on certain roads,
For fear of tripping on all the stones.

This is when a special friend steps forward
And quietly lends a hand.
We no longer have to walk alone,
And the stones are turned to sand.

There are many ways to lend a hand
And a friend always knows them all.
It's the deeds, as well as kind words,
That make a friend walk tall.

To me, Bill was a special friend,
Many times, he lent a hand.
He is one of those, I'll always remember,
As a kind and upright man.

TO MY FRIENDS

Thinking about my closest friends
Is a warm and loving thought -
And through the years I've been enriched,
By all the warmth it's brought.

Sharing memories, from time to time,
With those I hold so dear -
Are precious moments, in the pages of time,
That gently caress my ear.

Each generation invents new terms -
An esoteric language, to them alone.
Though I've learned the terms of five generations,
I can feel the warmth, when using my own.

And so, to all my friends both far and near,
I write these words so you will know -
Your friendship has meant a lot more to me,
Than any of the laurels, a king could bestow.

DEAN MAC

I've known this man for 28 years
And wish I'd known him before.
I can honestly say I always felt welcome
As I entered through his office door.

He came to Norwich around '36
And made his mark in the field of science.
His colleagues were to see the long suits of this man -
Fortitude, ambition, as well as reliance.

He told me of his courting days with Julie.
She was teaching school at the time.
He said he helped her with her math -
A noble calling for a man in his prime.

Late one night they were parking in a cemetery
When the caretaker sort of crossed their path.
Mac was asked just what he thought he was doing -
To which he replied, "I was helping this lady with her math."

Mac became Dean during my third year at Norwich.
He was truly the right man for the time.
As he moved into the office and arranged his pipes,
He knew there were mountains, he had to climb.

Director of continuing Education was my
Favorite Norwich job, thanks to my friend Mac.
He was my boss with a pile of patience -
Easing me along until I got the knack.

Mac appeared to believe in pulling rather
Than pushing, in order to get the job done.
Working for this man wasn't work at all -
His leadership made it fun.

He would stop by my office for a daily chat
And ask, "what are you planning for Norwich today?"
It was his way of "touching base"
And a friendly way, to start the day.

He always strived to make you feel comfortable -
Empathy? I believe he invented the word.
He could identify with most any problem
That one might have or might have heard.

One day I headed for his office to apologize
For not returning his call.
I suggested I was getting absent minded to which he
Replied," for the past five minutes I've been trying
To remember, just why I've been standing out in the hall."

Mac is one of the most unforgettable characters
In my life, one with a special blend.
He's been a great colleague and boss -
But more importantly, a super, super friend!

MORIN

I think of all the folks you've touched
And, skillfully, "turned some lives around."
Here's a tip of the hat, from a long - time friend,
To a fellow who's had both "feet on the ground."

We've both known those who like to talk -
They say very little, it's more like prattle.
I guess we could say they wear a big hat,
"But they never seem to have any cattle."

There're also those who go forth in this world
"Determined to set it on fire."
They seem to meander and aren't quite sure,
As to what it is they might aspire.

It takes all kinds to live in this world,
But it's rare when a leader is found.
Though some go forward and make a big "splash,"
I prefer the ones with "both feet on the ground."

Educators live forever,
Through the values they pass on.
Ideas seem to be the seeds of man
That grow and spread, long after we're gone.

There have been many times, in an Educator's world,
When ideas that were sown seemed to blow in the wind -
But sooner or later, some took root,
Minds opened up, ideas entered in.

When one can sow the ideas of man
Then blend with nature on a fishing trip -
Here is an educator with a handle on things,
Not holding with a grasp, but a solid grip!

And so my friend, you've made your mark
As you've worked and lived from town to town.
Once again, I salute you with a tip of my hat -
"To a close friend of mine with both feet on the ground."

CHAPLAIN JOHN

Throughout our lives, with all the toil,
There've been mountains we've had to climb.
We can only hope we've left a footprint,
To be duly recorded in the sands of time.

There are those, however, who've made numerous tracks
And should be applauded before they're gone.
I've known such a man and consider it a privilege,
To tell of my good friend, Chaplain John.

It's been a quarter of a century since our paths crossed,
I wish I had met him before.
He's a man with a definite goal in mind,
A man who obviously "knows the score."

I've watched him work with college students,
Also faculty and many, many more.
He was a tremendous asset to Norwich University,
And a strong supporter of the Cadets in the Corps.

It didn't seem to matter what he was doing
When a student came by with something to say.
They were all important and always welcome,
Whether five or ten minutes or the rest of the day.

One of the true measures of a person's worth
Is doing the job and going beyond.
I've never known a person more fitting of this,
Than my very, good friend, Chaplain John.

He's been extremely close to all of my family
And for that, I believe, we've all been blessed.
I pray that our faith will strengthen like his,
That we may be fulfilled when we lie down to rest.

As we witness the troubles around the world,
There are many who pray for a brand, new dawn.
I've often thought it was time to pray
For a lot more folks like Chaplain John.

BIRD HUNTIN'

Ced stopped by the other day
To do a little bird huntin', he and I.
It was a special, October day,
Hardly a cloud graced the sky.

We saw a few grouse, didn't get any,
In fact, we never fired a shot -
But the fellowship we shared outweighed
The chance of getting any game or not.

Hunting on grounds over which we had trod
For the past forty years or more -
Served as a catalyst to share experiences,
Otherwise known as hunter's lore.

As we walked down, past Poor Farm Gate
With its magnificent, wide, stone wall -
We discussed what it must've been like, two centuries ago.
In the distance, we heard a blue jay's call.

Though hidden, back in the hills of Peacham,
With trees growing from their cellar holes -
The remains of homes were eminently clear,
Telling a story that warmed our souls.

Stories were shared of our younger years
Of building a camp in the wood.
Traces could be seen of the trail that was made,
Leading to where the camp once stood.

Fellowship and memories make good therapy
As many so often claim.
A bird huntin' stroll, on a day in October,
Bolsters these values, making you glad you came.

HAL, A FRIEND AND NEIGHBOR

How many hearts does a pitcher touch,
Especially if the home town wins -
And how many players have been consoled
By the losing pitcher's grins?

How many students' lives were touched
By this teacher throughout the years?
How many frowns were turned to smiles?
How much comfort to those with tears?

It takes a special person, in times of crisis,
To answer his country's call -
But serving with honor, doing one's duty,
Is a way of standing tall.

With his love for music, singing in the chorus,
And friendship extended to all those within -
Memories were formed with a subtle touch
Accompanied by a friendly grin.

The St. Andrew's Society of Vermont
Will always remember his touch of grace.
Our Scottish heritage is a common bond,
One we cherish and dearly embrace.

Good friends and neighbors share many ties
Such as friendship, views and the like -
But Scots in Peacham have one more:
The love for a dry stane dyke.

And so we've lost a trusted friend,
One we'll miss with a saddened heart -
But the tracks he left are eminently
Clear: friendship to others both nigh and apart.

MY FRIEND ELMER

Elmer was a man of many talents
Who saw numerous mountains he needed to climb.
By so doing, he left countless footprints
Which were duly recorded in the sands of time.

I always enjoyed visiting with Elmer,
He was Mr. Vermont to me -
It was that practical, down to earth, willingness
To work - traits you so seldom see.

Seriousness of purpose?
He must have invented the term.
Every office he held was treated with respect
And was given his utmost concern.

As we prepared, each year, for the Kirkin O'
The Tartan, a lot of visiting took place.
Roping off the lawn was one of the jobs
And each stake, to Elmer, had a special place.

Working with Elmer, over the years,
Meeting House stories were rife.
I learned a great deal about its past -
Stories I'll treasure for the rest of my life.

It's impossible to measure this man's value
In all the service he gave to mankind -
But to put it in perspective, we need only to look,
At the loving family, he left behind.

Elmer Faris (seated) and Rev. Paul Wilson
Mosquitovile, VT

A CALEDONIA LEADER

When I stop to ponder of the ones I've known
And of all the mountains there've been to climb.
I thank my Maker for including me,
In the grandiose march of time.

It takes all kinds, I've heard it said,
To make up the world in which we live --
But it seems to me there are special folks
Who make lives better, by what they're willing to give.

When we think of giving
It's money that comes to mind.
Although it's important, we'd all agree,
There's a great deal more, we're destined to find.

A warm smile with a pleasant greeting
Does a great deal and takes little time.
It's a gesture we all can duly afford
And it doesn't cost a single dime.

A business person is often remembered
By the quality of service for which he stood.
Although more subtle, it is also remembered,
If he helped mankind wherever he could.

My friend Duncan is a point in case,
One we'll remember as the years pass by.
He ran a good business, square in his dealings,
Always friendly -- a right kind of guy.

Throughout northern Vermont and New Hampshire,
His farm equipment was sold.
For thirty years he served us well
Through the summer's heat and the winter's cold.

It was always comforting, knowing he was there,
When equipment problems arose.
He was a call away and very prompt,
As many a farmer knows.

He understood equipment crises
When a field of hay was ready to bale.
This was no time to "jig around,"
And certainly no time for a knotter to fail.

His machinery displays at the local fairs
Were always a special treat.
It gave us a chance to see the latest rigs
And made a good place for us boys to meet.

The contributions he's made to church and community,
While negotiating life's mountains there've been to climb-
Is surely testimonial to his ethical principles,
Thus leaving many footprints, in the sands of time.

DANCING AT THE LYNDON CORNER GRANGE

For over fifty years I've seen many changes
In the songs folks sing and the way they dance.
One has to wonder if these changes were planned,
Or did they just happen by some mere chance.

We have to look forward, as life goes on,
But it's nice to cling, a little to the past -
To favorite memories, special songs,
Certain times, and old dances that last.

There's an oasis in Lyndon, for folks like me,
Where we dance those steps that refuse to change.
The music, to which we dance, is endeared in our hearts,
As we dance with our memories, at the Lyndon Corner Grange.

Songs of the twenties, thirties and forties
With their rhythm, harmony and melodious charm -
Seem to work their magic of days gone by,
As we glide around the floor with her hand on my arm.

With Charlotte on the organ, Jim on his trumpet,
And close friends dancing on the floor -
There's an ambiance that prevails which is hard
To explain, music with memories and much, much more.

We all remember Leo playing his sax -
He also had a smile that never seemed to change.
We all felt sad when his time finally came,
He's very much missed at the Lyndon Corner Grange

Mildred and Lilla are always there
To greet you every Saturday night.
Their duties are those of a Maitre-de,
Rendered with a smile that's sheer delight.

This dance at the Grange has quite a tradition,
Operating for a century or so.
The reason it lasted is dedicated people -
Folks who are interested in making it go.

Many have heard Charlotte play the organ
With fingers that seem to fly.
She has a treasury of songs stored in her head,
Music of today and of days gone by.

We were new in town and searching a little -
You might say, looking for a change.
We were delighted to find this "gem in the green"
And dance with these folks, at the Lyndon Corner Grange.

Nature has a way of granting rewards
To those who try and her arms embrace.
One can sense this bit of magic
As he passes by my neighbor's place.

MY NEIGHBOR'S PLACE

It's just down the road a piece,
Over to my neighbor's place -
His jerseys are out to pasture,
An idyllic scene, with a touch of grace.

I hear them lowing from time to time -
A contented sound, with a bit of charm.
If he was asked about his lifestyle preference,
I reckon he'd say, "I'd rather farm."

It's a lot of hard work and the hours are long,
Working from dawn 'til dark -
But there's satisfaction, owning your place,
And knowing full well you're making a mark.

There's not the cacophony of the city
Or the push of the crowds "through a funnel."
It's a pleasant walk, along a dirt road,
Under the maples' majestic tunnel.

There's a time to sow and a time to reap
While one eye is fixed on the weather.
Sometimes your right other times your wrong.
Every once in awhile, your luck can be balanced with a feather.

Nature has a way of granting rewards
To those who try and her arms embrace.
One can sense this bit of magic
As he passes by my neighbor's place.

SPECIAL FOLKS IN GREEN BAY

Every once-in-awhile some folks come along
With a certain talent and a special flair.
They're the kind you like for really close neighbors -
Folks who make you glad they're there.

Dick and Dottie are folks like this -
A couple who enjoy their home in Green Bay.
They're molding this homestead with a labor of love -
"Bringing the past to the present," I've heard some say.

There's a susurrant ambience that seems to prevail
As you survey what they've done with this home of the past.
Time takes its toll, causing signs of wear -
But the glorious signs that meet your eye,
Are the results of loving hands, that made it last.

It's been said, "knowing where we've been
And what we've done, helps us decide where we shall go."
Knowledge of the past renders comfort and strength -
And it's folks like the Hoveys that help make it so.

As they wander around their bucolic grounds
They can view the White Mountains -
A magnificent sight to see.
Though these mountains belong to the state of New Hampshire,
They can say to themselves,
"The view belongs to me."

What a treasure they've developed, what a legacy they'll leave -
As they forge their footprints in the sands of time.
They're retiring from the world of hustle and bustle
For a home in Green Bay, and another big mountain to climb.

MY FRIEND SID

I have a close friend with whom I visit,
We've always known him as Sid.
Our visits often center about the past,
How people lived and what they did.

Here's a man who will leave a footprint -
He's already written a book.
It's about the past of his hometown
And the way that Chelsea used to look.

It would be an injustice, attempting to list
The accomplishments of this special man.
Most would agree he's a super citizen -
Always available to lend a hand.

To know where we've been, from whence we came,
A detailed knowledge of the past -
Provides us with hope, a guiding light,
And a strong resolve, to make things last.

If anyone has forged a footprint in time,
Describing Chelsea and what its citizens did -
There is truly one, standing extra tall,
Let's have a round of applause, for my friend Sid.

The information that he's recording
Will be priceless as time goes on.
They'll be talking about this man's footprints
A long time after he's gone.

As we go through this life we meet lots of folks
And reflect, sometimes, about what they did.
I've never seen a man who loves his hometown
Nearly as much as my friend Sid.

MY FRIEND BEANIE

There comes a time in all our lives,
To reflect on the mountains we've had to climb.
Our footprints are noted, as life goes forward,
And duly recorded in the sands of time.

Nearly fifty years have come and gone
Since we wore the suits of red and gold.
Thousands applauded as we marched and played,
Creating a saga, that needs to be told.

We each had our place where we marched and played,
And knew all were needed in this special band.
So it is with each, in the lives we live -
And so it was in life, with this special man.

Beanie, with his sousaphone, marched up front,
Playing with zest, which was heard by all.
In between marches, there was a smile on his face.
Here was a person, who really stood tall.

I have to believe we each have a mission,
As we march and play in life's special band.
Harmony and friendship were important to Beanie,
Listening to others, to understand.

We are often exposed, in this society of ours,
To a cacophony of sounds that fill the air.
Who is to say? There just might be a
Little more harmony, and we'll all know -
That Beanie was there.

MY FRIEND DONNY

I'd like to share a story about a friend of mine -
He was a wiry, nimble, little man.
One could say he put a lot into life,
Even though he had one hand.

He could play a fiddle, as well as repair it,
And expertly, string a bow.
How it was done with just one hand,
Was a marvel to watch, I'll have you know.

Donny painted houses and drove the stage,
Grew a fine garden and sugared each year.
Of all the hunting he ever did,
I believe his favorite, was the Whitetail Deer.

There was a notch in his gun for each deer he'd taken -
They were notches of pride for this little man.
When asked why the notches in the butt of his gun -
He replied, "the gun won't slip from my hand."

The sense of humor, this fellow had,
Was endless and something to behold.
He'll be remembered around Chelsea for a long, long time,
For what he did and the stories he told.

On a slushy, dreary day, late in the winter,
As folks complained about the weather the season would bring,
Along would come Donny, whistling a tune,
Then say, "this is good weather, it's great for my spring!"

Donny and I hunted and fished,
I believe I could write a book.
It seemed each time we ever went fishing,
The fish would end up on Donny's hook.

Instead of going to church on a Sunday morning,
He often could be seen, mowing someone's lawn.
The service was free, this was his good deed,
He's very much missed, now that he's gone.

A number of times, I've heard him exclaim
As we hunted in the woods, early in the day -
"Look at all this wonder that so many are missing,
By staying in bed on such a beautiful day."

I've hunted and hiked with a number of folks
And enjoyed the company of them all -
But of all the folks who've walked in the woods,
It's this nimble, little man who stands real tall.

Heaven, to Donny, would be woods for hunting,
Where the season is never done.
If it's so, and I think it is,
There'll be another notch in the butt of his gun.

Pheasant hunt with Donny.

119

MY BROTHER RAY

Since he and I were much younger than the rest of the family,
We played together in the early years.
There were happy times during the Depression
As well as those with tears.

East Hill, Peacham was where we were born -
On a small subsistence farm.
A dog, cats, cows, horses and chickens were our friends -
Which, in a way added a touch of charm.

There was a small stream that trickled by,
Something small boys cannot resist.
The dams we built and toy boats we made
Were only a part of our innovative list.

Some of the maples, under which we played,
Still remain to this very day.
How they survived the '38 hurricane,
Is something that's hard to say.

September twenty-first of '38 was a frightening time
As we huddled together in the dining room.
The howl of the wind was a treacherous sound,
As each of us considered our doom.

We could hear our buildings being torn apart
First our silo and barn, then a little closer by.
Dad mentioned "we might be in trouble
If the chimney blew off" -- little Ray began to cry.

The next morning we surveyed the damage
Then counted our blessings for being alive.
Better things were to come,
We had a will to survive.

Ray and I attended school at East Hill
In the Fall of 38.
Shortly after the hurricane we moved to South Peacham.
With the storm for a reference -
It's easy to remember the date.

120

The school seats and desk were not adjustable.
To get a fit, for little guys, was an academic chore.
The teacher placed a box under Ray's feet
So he could make contact with the schoolhouse floor.

In the Spring of '39 we moved to McIndoe Falls
Onto a farm named "Bonnie View."
A beautiful farm by the Connecticut River,
Truly, a gorgeous view.

It was here we grew up with many friends
That have lasted over the years.
There are lots of memories that both of us have
And times we hold so dear.

There was Indian Knoll
That had a mystique and touched
A young fellow's mind.
We were never quite sure,
With a little bit of digging, just
What our efforts might find.

The swimming hole was a gathering place
On hot and muggy days.
We had all helped in making the dam,
In various and sundry ways.

The campsite was extra special
For tenting over night.
Stories were told around the campfire -
Memories provide a tranquil sight.

We both joined the Boy Scouts,
Barnet Troop number one.
Ski hikes, swimming, boating, canoeing,
Zack Woods Scout Camp, North Wolcott, Vt.
Taught us how things should be done.

Living near the Connecticut River,
Its backwater canals and ponds -
Was enough to whet a young fellows taste,
For boats, fishing, trapping and beyond.

The war years involved us all-
Our older brother, Leon, was in the army
And badly wounded, outside of Manilla,
But he survived and returned home after
The war--thank God for that.

On the home-front we were highly involved
Collecting scrap metal, paper, and
Practicing Air Raid Drills in school.

The village practiced blackout drills
And just to avoid dispel,
The signals went out from our local church,
Our Dad rang the bell. (Ray and I "helped").

After the war we took music lessons,
Ray played the trombone, I the Cornet,
We made a musical pair,
By playing for company and Christmas
In Church, we developed a special flare.

We were then ready for bigger things
Or at least a different brand.
What we would experience would shape our lives,
We played in McLure's Band.

The band is where Ray met Ginny
With whom he's been married
For more than fifty years.
To them I say "God Bless you both,
And many, many cheers!

Our East Hill Home
Peacham, Vermont
Ray is sitting on Dad's lap
I'm sitting as close as I can
1934

April On Mack's Mountain

I walked around the grounds, this April day,
To see the remains of winter on our lawn.
Birds were singing as though welcoming spring,
Most of the snow was gone.

There seemed to be a freshness in the air
As though a new dawn had sprung.
Tree branches seemed to bow their heads -
A result, perhaps, of where the snow had clung.

I find it refreshing, as time moves on,
To welcome the seasons as they take their turn.
Each one seems to have a rebirth,
But there's always something new to learn.

Mack's Mountain weather can be tricky,
Especially this time of year.
It just might rain then turn to snow -
Or it might cloud up then come off clear.

Whether it's rain, snow or sunshine,
Our feathered friends come and go.
Some change color and sing new songs,
Spring has sprung - each one of them seems to know.

A PEACHAM MIRACLE ?

Perhaps it was the pre-Christmas season,
For Christmas was but five days away.
I believe I saw a miracle
As I attended church that day.

Small children conducted the service,
Their faces were all aglow.
I observed with a grandfather's interest
As I sat with Grammie, in the fifth row.

For all the times I've heard the Christmas story,
I know the lines by heart -
But the story was new to these little folks
And their eagerness showed, as each one played a part.

There was a little boy standing out front
With his hands in his pockets and grinning from ear to ear.
A very little girl strolling around the pulpit,
Not saying a word, but looking ever so dear.

There were some, a little bit older, who
Were obviously eager to sing.
They also guided the little ones around -
Who weren't quite as sure, also prone to cling.

As the children shed their animal costumes.
The pastor pretended to awake from a dream.
He told of all the little animals he'd seen
And how real, to him, they actually seemed.

The squeals of delight told the story -
For a moment they had "lived" the part.
It was enough to moisten Grampa's eye
And tenderly touch Grandma's heart.

THE PICTURE AT CVH

A Broadwing dipped his wings
As he soared in the morning air.
Two pigeons nervously banked and swerved,
Knowing full well why the hawk was there.

A small wispy cloud rode a gentle breeze
And appeared to nod as it drifted by.
Spruce Mountain majestically stood in the distance
All part of my view from CVH
That magically caught my eye.

Way in the distance, smoke was rising -
Activity in a sugar house, I imagined the reason
Though the day was the Sabbath, there was the last of the run
That had to be boiled, to clean things up,
And "wrap up the season."

Turning from the window of CVH
And focusing on the hubbub, going on inside -
There was a hustle and bustle by these folks of mercy,
As their arts of healing were being applied.

It is comforting to know, in time of need,
There are folks in this world who really care.
Surely these folks will be justly rewarded -
Though we don't know when,
And we don't know where.

I believe our Maker is taking notice and keeping score,
As he records their footprints in the sands of time.
A just reward for these folks of mercy,
As they deal with life and its mountains
They have to climb.

Written as a patient in
Central Vermont Hospital.

DAYS OF GRACE

I've been retired nigh onto sixteen years,
It's amazing how time has flown.
I'm thankful for the health of our family,
The grandchildren are nearly full grown.

Bonnie View has provided a special haven
Where the mind can ponder of natural things -
Like where the sun rises and where the moon sets,
What the sparrow eats, and the song it sings.

We like to think and dearly hope,
A mark was made in our working life.
What I am and what I did,
I truly owe to my loving wife.

Our lives are now busy, but very content,
As we work together throughout the year.
Our sense of direction seems to be guided
Without the concern, of who's going to steer.

There's no question we're blessed with what we have -
It's our family we lovingly embrace.
As the weeks fly by, we become aware,
We're living in days of grace.

FLOWERS AND MUSIC

Music flows around Bonnie View
When the girls sing with their Mother.
The harmony they create is Heaven sent,
Also complimentary to one another.

I make it a point to stay out of sight,
But well within my hearing range.
It's time to lean back and enjoy myself
And just relax for a change.

Their voices have a rare blend
That's been refined throughout the years.
The kind, if you please, that waters your eyes,
Otherwise known as musical tears.

She taught them to sing, early in life,
As they forged ahead on the road of trials.
They came to see what music can do,
As one travels along with musical miles.

I've heard it said that Angels sing
Somewhere way up high.
I believe my three girls have developed a preempt.
I can feel it in my eyes.

128

TO BILL AND ROXIE

I've crossed my fingers, dearly hoped,
And at times I even pray --
That for all you've done and all you've helped,
A lot of nice things will come your way.

Being patient isn't easy when life is pressing
And you're "operating up to your nose."
Some will say, "that's simply life"
Or, "that's the way it goes."

It is, in fact, only the special,
The ones who are always there -
Those, if you please, looking out for others,
The folks who really care.

I thank my Maker for special folks
Who touch so many, before they're through.
They appear to have a noble quest,
And hearts that are nobly true.

My hat is off to you gentle people
For all the nice things you do.
There are many, I'm sure, sharing this thought:
"If only there were more like you!"

TO OUR SON STEVE

Since the day you were born
Your Mother and I have watched with pride.
You have a way of facing the world,
Going forth with a measured stride.

As far back as we can remember
You have always had lots of friends,
From the time you made Eagle Scout to
Professional work, the list has had no end.

You have always been considerate,
Ready to lend a hand.
Quick to weigh the issues
Before you take a stand.

It soon became eminently clear
That you truly were born to lead.
We often speak of the lives you've touched,
Guiding them to meet a need.

To see you nurture your children
And knowing how much you care -
Has been heart warming to us
And an answer to a prayer.

TO RICH AND SHARON

The years have slowly dimmed my eyes,
But I'm thankful for what they see.
It's folks like you, helping so many -
A heart warming sight, and pleasing to me.

The path of life gets strewn with pebbles,
There are those who attempt to block your way -
But a steadfast resolve to do what's right,
Is a noble goal that brightens the day.

You may never receive all the verbal thanks
That folks like you deserve -
But thanks come to us in many ways,
It depends on how you observe.

Winning is important, a few losses don't hurt,
We strive to smile with pride.
What's really important is not winning or losing,
But how we feel inside.

And so it is with these old eyes -
I've made known, just what they see.
It's caring folks, like the two of you,
Making a difference, to what the future will be.

55 YEARS AGO

The Midshipmen of
McIndoes Academy

Front Row L to R :Leslie (Bucky) Conant; Wendall Powers;
Melvin Somers; Carlisle (Mike) Griffin; Carroll Brown; Paul Bedell
Back Row L to R: Rev. Bill Hudson, Coach; Donald Dickinson;
Gilbert Theroux; Kenneth Emery; Raymond Somers

Tempus fugit, as the saying goes,
It's amazing how time flies by.
Though half a century has come and gone
The memories abide behind my eye.

As I look at this picture of long ago
And see the pride in all our eyes -
I think of the values all of us gained,
The camaraderie, fellowship, and teammate ties.

We had a good year, as seasons go,
Sporting a record of nineteen and three -
But the coach taught more than playing the game,
Or it's the way it seemed to me.

132

Most all of us attended the coach's fellowship meetings,
Which were held every Sunday night.
I can't really say what the incentive was -
Perhaps the girls in attendance, helped shed a little light.

We won the Hilldale League trophy.
A highly coveted prize -
But there was a lot more around the corner
That "opened" a number of eyes.

The Wells River Kiwanis tournament,
At the time, was the talk of the town.
Once more the Middies struck pay dirt
And walked off with the tournament crown.

Next was the Monroe, Men's Club tournament
We knew it was "do or die."
The final was close as some had predicted,
But the Middies, again, squeaked by.

In March of '49 the Middies were invited to St. Johnsbury
For competition with Derby, St. J. and L.I.
Though the smallest school there, we garnered the trophy,
Then headed south with heads held high!

There's been ample time for numerous thoughts,
A lot of snow has come and gone -
Far more was gained than winning the games,
As values were instilled, to go above and beyond.

Epilogue:

The Hilldale League was formed in the school year 1947 - 48 with
membership including the following secondary schools:
Danville High School, Concord High School, St. Johnsbury Trade
School, Peacham Academy, McIndoes Academy, Wells River High School,
Newbury High School and Groton High School
Other league activities included one act play contests, combined chorus
concert, baseball and a Grand Ball in the spring of the year.

McIndoes Academy
Founded 1853

Though small in numbers, it had an
enviable record of producing leaders
from both far and near.

Chelsea Red Devil Band

From time to time I stop to think
As well as reminisce.
I find it rewarding, also fulfilling -
Similar, I think, to my spouse's kiss.

Among the highlights of all my thoughts,
To tell precisely where I stand -
Are the hours I spent, giving lessons,
And putting together a marching band.

The Chelsea Red Devils were very young
But very determined and strong of heart.
Each one seemed determined to learn -
They all were eager, to do their part.

Town folks turned out to hear them play
And watch them go through their drills.
Tunbridge Fair was on their list
With all of its flair and thrills.

Once the word got around
They were booked for out of town.
Various concerts also parades
Folks marveled, at their precision and sound.

The Eastern States Exposition appeared on their list,
Truly a prestigious goal!
But more important was the pride instilled,
And the memorable stories told.

The Chelsea Red Devils were very young
But very determined and strong of heart.
Each one seemed determined to learn -
They all were eager, to do their part.